School Councils across Europe

Moral Development and Citizenship Education

Series Editors

Wiel Veugelers (*University of Humanistic Studies, Utrecht, The Netherlands*)
Kirsi Tirri (*University of Helsinki, Finland*)

Founding Editor

Fritz Oser†

Editorial Board

Nimrod Aloni (*Kibbutzim College of Education, Tel Aviv, Israel*)
Marvin Berkowitz (*University of Missouri–St. Louis, USA*)
Horst Biedermann (*St. Gallen University of Teacher Education, Switzerland*)
Maria Rosa Buxarrais (*University of Barcelona, Spain*)
Helen Haste (*University of Bath, UK/Harvard University, USA*)
Dana Moree (*Charles University, Prague, Czech Republic*)
Clark Power (*University of Notre Dame, USA*)
Jasmine Sim (*National Institute of Education, Singapore*)
Joel Westheimer (*University of Ottawa, Canada*)

VOLUME 22

The titles published in this series are listed at *brill.com/mora*

School Councils across Europe

Democratic Forums or Exclusive Clubs?

By

Isabel Kempner and Jan Germen Janmaat

BRILL

LEIDEN | BOSTON

Cover illustration: *Looking In*, © Gillian Holding, 2022

All chapters in this book have undergone peer review.

The Library of Congress Cataloging-in-Publication Data is available online at https://catalog.loc.gov

Typeface for the Latin, Greek, and Cyrillic scripts: "Brill". See and download: brill.com/brill-typeface.

ISSN 2352-5770
ISBN 978-90-04-54136-8 (paperback)
ISBN 978-90-04-54133-7 (hardback)
ISBN 978-90-04-54137-5 (e-book)

Copyright 2023 by Koninklijke Brill NV, Leiden, The Netherlands.
Koninklijke Brill NV incorporates the imprints Brill, Brill Nijhoff, Brill Hotei, Brill Schöningh, Brill Fink, Brill mentis, Vandenhoeck & Ruprecht, Böhlau, V&R unipress and Wageningen Academic.
All rights reserved. No part of this publication may be reproduced, translated, stored in a retrieval system, or transmitted in any form or by any means, electronic, mechanical, photocopying, recording or otherwise, without prior written permission from the publisher. Requests for re-use and/or translations must be addressed to Koninklijke Brill NV via brill.com or copyright.com.

This book is printed on acid-free paper and produced in a sustainable manner.

Contents

Preface VII
List of Figures and Tables VIII

1 **Introduction: Access to School Councils** 1

2 **Democratic Forums** 4
   1   What Are School Councils? 4
   2   The Normative Justification 6
   3   The Pedagogical Justification 7
   4   Contextualising School Councils within Citizenship Education 10
   5   Case Studies 12
   6   Discussion of the Case Studies 17
   7   Why School Councils? 22
   8   Chapter Summary 23

3 **Questions of Access** 24
   1   National Level 24
   2   School Level 28
   3   Individual Level 31

4 **A Quantitative Approach** 38
   1   Data Source 38
   2   Variables 40
   3   Method 45

5 **Results: Determinants of Access to School Councils across Europe** 47
   1   The Empty Model 47
   2   Country Level Analysis 47
   3   School Level Analysis 50
   4   Initial Observations at the Individual Level 53
   5   Determinants of Individuals' Participation (Multi-Level Analysis) 55

6 **Exclusive Clubs** 61
    1   International Overview 61
    2   The Influence of Political Cultures 63
    3   The Influence of School Type 64
    4   The Influence of Socio-Demographic Characteristics 66
    5   The Implications of Our Findings 69

7 **Improving Democratic Education** 73

Appendix: Full Wording and Coding from the ICCS Questionnaires for All Applicable Variables 77
References 80
Index 90

Preface

In the face of a perceived decline in political participation amongst young people, the European Union Youth Strategy (2019–2027) identifies a need to create space for all young people to develop a political voice. The literature on citizenship education highlights school councils as a promising initiative to address this goal. School councils aim to be democratic decision-making forums for students at school. While there has been much research on the outcomes of these councils, there seem to be very few studies examining who has access to them. The purpose of this study is to analyse patterns of access to school councils in order to more clearly understand how this form of citizenship education may be perpetuating political inequalities.

At the heart of this book is an analysis of quantitative data from the International Association for the Evaluation of Educational Achievement's (IEA) International Civic and Citizenship Education Study (ICCS). We investigate the characteristics associated with participation in school councils across Europe. The research questions interrogate access at three levels: national, school and individual. Do pupils in different countries, schools, and with certain socio-demographic characteristics have differential access to participation opportunities on the school council? Does this differential access reflect pre-existing patterns in inequitable political participation in wider society?

The results of this analysis reveal worrying inequalities in access at all three levels. We argue that the patterns apparent in school council access both reflect, and perpetuate, political inequalities found in societies across Europe. This book will therefore be of interest to all those concerned with the role of education systems in building a fair and democratic society, such as teachers, researchers and policy-makers in the fields of citizenship and comparative education. In order to ensure that all young people develop a political voice, it is first important to understand where inequalities may exist. This book contributes to a growing body of evidence on inequalities in access to citizenship education.

Figures and Tables

Figures

1 Percentage of schools with a council within each country and political culture. 48
2 Proportion of schools (with 95% confidence intervals) with a council within five political cultures. 49
3 Predicted probability of having a school council by school type (1). 51
4 Predicted probability of having a school council by school type (2). 52
5 Bivariate associations between pupil characteristics and participation on the school council. 54

Tables

1 Re-code of DV2 into binary dependent variable. 41
2 Country groupings for the variable 'political culture'. 41
3 Descriptive data for all dependent and independent variables. 44
4 Determinants of school council availability at the school level. 50
5 Determinants of individuals' participation on the school council in EU countries. 56
6 Determinants of individuals' participation on the school council in five countries. 57

CHAPTER 1

Introduction

Access to School Councils

It has long been argued that schooling serves a wider purpose than merely teaching academic subjects. Education has historically been a key tool for influencing the social order and, in this sense, schools are thought to have a civic dimension (Campbell, 2008). Schools are expected to transfer the foundations of society from one generation to the next (Walther, 2012). However, in this role, schools potentially have the power both to perpetuate social inequalities and to correct them. In more recent times, a major focus in educational research has been on how schools can be used to disrupt the social order. That is, researchers have explored how education can aid social mobility (e.g. Breen & Müller, 2020; Great Britain, Department for Education, 2017). Yet the bulk of the research on this topic has focused on academic attainment and success, while the civic dimension of schooling has been notably under-researched (Hoskins, Janmaat, & Melis, 2017) and overshadowed by a narrow focus on academic attainment (Campbell, 2008). It is thought that this civic aspect of schooling has the potential to create a more just society by ensuring that all pupils are equally well-equipped to engage with their role as citizens and by reducing existing inequalities in civic knowledge and behaviours (Bischoff, 2016). In this book, we therefore hope to add to the literature on how education can be used to create a more just society, with a particular focus on citizenship. We aim to do this by highlighting a way in which schools might be inadvertently reflecting and reproducing political inequalities in society: through unequal access to school councils.

The political engagement of the youth population is high on the agenda of politicians and researchers in the face of a perceived decline in participation (European Commission, 2009). In many elections in countries across the EU, youth have the lowest voter turnout compared with other age groups (Kitanova, 2019). The EU considers this extremely problematic: participation is seen as the most important principle of democracy (Council of Europe, 2020). Young people have therefore become a target for political participation. It is in this context that the EU developed its Youth Strategy (European Union, 2018). As part of this strategy, European Youth Goal 9 states the need to promote 'Space and Participation for All'. More specifically, it is to 'strengthen young people's democratic participation and autonomy as well as provide dedicated youth spaces in all areas of society' (ibid., p. 15). The fact that participation is stipulated to be for *all* strongly implies a concern with political equality between different groups. The EU's idea of participation encompasses, but goes beyond, traditional modes of engagement such as voting and standing for elections. It also includes influencing decisions, engaging in actions and contributing to building a better society (Council of Europe, 2015). In this book, political participation is conceived of in this broad sense: it is about active citizenship in order to shape society.

Bringing together the civic dimension of schooling and this current problem facing EU democracies, schools in member states of the EU are thought to be a promising starting point for addressing youth participation (European Commission, 2017). It is considered both their responsibility and their remit to promote space and participation for all (Walther, 2012). One initiative gaining increasing popularity across Europe is the school council, which provides a democratic forum for pupils to make decisions on matters that affect them.

Yet there is a need to investigate how school councils do – or do not – address European Youth Goal 9. Previous research on school councils has focused on their impact and effects (e.g. Torney-Purta et al., 2001; Perry, 2011; Keating & Janmaat, 2016; Hoskins & Janmaat, 2019). There has been little research on how *differential access* to school councils might impact on their ability to provide space and promote participation for all. Two studies of note suggest that access may be a salient issue. Research conducted by McFarland and Starmanns (2009) and, separately, Kahne and Middaugh (2008a, 2008b) reveals differences in the civic participation opportunities offered by schools in the USA. These studies provide evidence that access to such opportunities may be unequal between individuals with different socio-economic characteristics and between schools with different student body compositions. This suggests a need to consider patterns of access to school councils at the level of both the individual and the school. Moreover, the existing research focuses only on schools and individuals in the USA. There is a need to consider access issues in Europe and, since Europe is composed of many countries, it is also important to consider differential access between countries. Keating's (2014) research on citizenship education in Europe highlights the need to consider how EU member states may respond in different and diverse ways to EU-wide goals, of which European Youth Goal 9 is an example. Since member states retain control over their education systems, it is possible that civic participation opportunities may vary between countries (ibid.). Our focus is on which pupils, in which schools and countries, have access to school councils. Unlike most existing research, we will not be empirically investigating the outcomes of school councils, although we will discuss likely outcomes in the literature review in order to understand the consequences of unequal access.

Our research questions are therefore as follows:
1. Do pupils in countries across the EU have equal access to school councils?
2. Do pupils in different schools have equal access to school councils?
3. Do individuals within those schools have equal access to school councils?

In order to address our research questions, we will begin by establishing a theoretical basis and motivation for the study. In Chapter 2, *Democratic Forums*, we will present the theory behind school councils found in the pre-existing literature on the topic. In this way, we will draw out how school councils are thought to address European Youth Goal 9. This must be established first in order for uneven access to then be problematised in the remainder of the book. In Chapter 3, *Questions of Access*, we will explore the theoretical barriers to political participation – both in society and in schools – for various groups at the national, school and individual levels. On the basis of this discussion, we will formulate our hypotheses regarding which groups or individuals face reduced access to school councils.

The book will then move from theory to empirical research as we use SPSS (IBM Corp, 2017) to analyse quantitative survey data from the International Association for the Evaluation of Educational Achievement's (IEA) International Civic and Citizenship Education Study (ICCS). Using these data, we aim to explore the influence of various factors on access to school councils. We will explain our data source, variables and methods in Chapter 4 and then present the results of our analyses in Chapter 5. In Chapter 6, *Exclusive Clubs,* we question the extent to which school councils across Europe are currently addressing European Youth Goal 9 and counteracting political inequalities. The data will underpin a discussion on whether schools are acting as sites for societal progress, or tools for perpetuating society as it already exists. We will conclude in Chapter 7 by drawing some tentative conclusions on this theme, based on the empirical research on access to school councils.

This book may be of interest to those who are concerned with the role of education systems in building a fair and democratic society. In particular, our findings are relevant to teachers, researchers and policy-makers in the field of citizenship and democratic education; the implications for policy and practice are discussed in our concluding chapter. Since we take an international, comparative approach in our research questions, students and researchers of comparative education and comparative politics may also find this book of use.

CHAPTER 2

Democratic Forums

1   What Are School Councils?

School councils are organisations in schools that represent the views and interests of the student body (Cross, Hulme, & McKinney, 2014). They aim to provide a 'formal, democratic, transparent, accountable, whole-school policy forum' (Alderson, 2000, p. 124). Each of these adjectives is illuminating but 'democratic' is perhaps the key one; school councils provide a forum for pupils to have a say in matters that affect them. The Eurydice (2017) report on Citizenship Education emphasises the contrast with the average classroom environment, which is teacher-led. School councils can be found across the world, in both primary and secondary schools, in both academic and vocational streams.

Given the broad range of contexts in which school councils exist, it is to be expected that they vary in terms of structure, organisation, decision-making power and purpose. This is certainly the case. However, there are fundamental similarities between school councils, particularly within Europe, which underpin our discussion of school councils in this book. In this chapter, we aim to give an overview of the theory and practice of school councils, recognising the variety that exists, but also identifying important similarities.

As a forum for students to have a say in issues that affect them, we exclude from our discussion school councils that do not include any students. So-called school councils without any student representation can be found, often in the USA, often involving community members with the aim of school improvement (e.g. Medina et al., 2020; Pharis, Bass, & Pate, 2005). These councils are not the topic of this book. Of those councils that do include pupils, there are some that include only pupils; these are often referred to as 'student councils' or 'pupil councils'. Others are composed of a range of different stakeholders, including students, teachers, parents and governors. In this book, our discussion encompasses both of these types of school councils. This was necessary because the ICCS dataset provides data only on whether or not a school has a council, and whether a student is a representative on a council; it does not provide descriptive data on what kind of council this is.

We use this broad definition reluctantly, since student-only school councils may better meet the demands of European Youth Goal 9. Hart's (1992, p. 8) ladder of participation provides a theoretical framework for considering pupil participation in decision-making. At one end of the continuum is manipulation, which can be considered the opposite of genuine pupil participation: it is when adults control the decision-making process but pupils are used as a mouthpiece for their views. Whitty and Wisby (2007b) emphasise a risk of pupil voice being used merely to legitimise the actions of adults in power; there is more potential for this to happen with adults involved in the council. At the opposite end of Hart's ladder, there is child-initiated decision-making that is shared between adults and pupils. This truly subverts the usual authoritarian power dynamic of a school, as pupils control who is invited into the decision-making process. It seems likely that a school council with less adult involvement will be more in line with European Youth Goal 9, which specifies the need to strengthen young people's democratic autonomy.

The fact that we must include both student-only and mixed stakeholder councils is not a major problem for two reasons. First and foremost, the main topic of this book is *access* to school councils. For the purposes of our discussion, we aim to establish only that school councils have the potential to meet European Youth Goal 9, in order to highlight the likely consequences of inequality in access. School councils involving adults as well as students may also meet European Youth Goal 9, but potentially to a lesser extent. Second, it seems that student-only councils are more common than other kinds of school councils. Mager and Nowak (2012) carried out a systematic review of the literature on the effects of student participation in decision-making processes in schools. They categorise different types of student participation in decision-making and find that student-only school councils are by far the most common structure for student decision-making in schools. This finding is corroborated by much of the literature on school councils within Europe, with school councils 'usually involving elected student representatives' (Eurydice, 2017, p. 79). We therefore include mixed-stakeholder councils with the proviso that these seem to constitute only a minority of the school councils in Europe.

We have established that school councils are supposed to be decision-making forums and an opportunity for pupils to have their voice heard. We turn now to the purpose of such forums. We identify two common justifications for school councils, which provide the theoretical underpinning for their discussion. These are the normative and pedagogical justifications (Keating & Janmaat, 2016). These two approaches appear to consider children at two different stages of their citizenship journeys. While the former addresses the rights of pupils as present citizens, the latter addresses the needs of pupils as future citizens. Both justifications link school councils with European Youth Goal 9 – providing space and participation to all – but at different times. We will explore each justification in turn to show how each relates to European Youth Goal 9.

2 The Normative Justification

The normative justification for school councils considers pupils as current citizens, with corresponding rights and responsibilities. In this way, 'school councils are a key practical and symbolic indicator of respect for children's rights' (Alderson, 2000, p. 124). European Youth Goal 9 speaks to a key aspect of any democratic society: people should have the space to participate in decision-making and have their voice heard. Thornberg and Elvstrand (2012) have identified a tension between this fundamental requirement of a democracy and the typically authoritarian structure of schools. Education systems tend to have a strict hierarchy, where adults at the top have the power to make decisions and students are powerless (Schugurensky, 2006). A school council, then, might be considered a way of disrupting this undemocratic structure in order to assure pupils' rights.

Taking the normative viewpoint, some have suggested that schools should be regarded as microcosms of society and mini democracies (Amnå, 2012). What kind of democracy, though, might a school with a school council represent? Dubet (2013) distinguishes between representative and participatory democracy. While the key driver of representative democracy is to shape projects to reflect the interests of relevant parties, participatory democracy responds to a 'democratic imperative that compels every individual to be involved and participate in the democratic purpose' (ibid., p. 147). The latter is clearly a more radical conception of democracy in requiring the active involvement of every individual, rather than just the consideration of everyone's interests. Examples of pupil involvement in participatory democracy at schools do exist (e.g. Kirshner & Jefferson, 2015). However, school councils, as described in this book, tend *not* to involve the active participation of every individual. Rather, a few representatives are tasked with shaping school life according to the interests and needs of the wider pupil body. In this sense, school councils might be considered as efforts to promote representative democracy.

Yet, equally, school councils tend to respond only very weakly to a description of a representative democracy. In an educational setting (Higher Education), De Boer and Stensaker (2007) highlight three key features of representative democracies. First, key stakeholders have the right to elect representatives, and are themselves eligible to be elected; second, these representatives have substantial powers, including power over the budget; and third, decision-making powers are distributed fairly evenly. In reality, school councils are likely to fulfil the first criterion but correspond less to the final two as schools may be reluctant to grant such power to young pupils (Cox & Robinson-Pant, 2005; McFarland & Starmanns, 2009; Burnitt & Gunter, 2013). It would appear, then, that a normative justification for school councils sees their purpose fulfilled only partly. They cannot be classified easily as examples of participatory or representative democracy.

Although a school council may not exemplify a model of democracy found at the national level, it may tap key democratic principles and in that way fulfil its role under the normative justification (McCowan & Unterhalter, 2013). In particular, school councils offer opportunities for democratic *participation*. There is some dispute over the extent to which school councils provide participation opportunities corresponding to the higher rungs of Hart's (1992) ladder of participation (Whitty & Wisby, 2007a). However, we can imagine a school council that would, with students inviting adults into the decision-making forum. Thus school councils, at their best, can theoretically be justified on normative grounds: they provide an opportunity for democratic participation for the representatives on the council. They do not, however, provide this opportunity to those who are not representatives, which raises the issue of access: a point to which we will return.

In summary, the normative justification for school councils considers schools as micro societies and pupils as present – not just future – citizens. If this is accepted, then it would follow that, in a democratic society, a school council is a necessary organisational body to respond to European Youth Goal 9.

3   The Pedagogical Justification

The pedagogical justification has also been called the empirical justification (Keating & Janmaat, 2016), highlighting the *outcomes* as important, and moving away from the idea that councils are intrinsically justified. Rather, councils are thought to be justified in their role as *learning* tools and are an aspect of citizenship education (Hoskins, Janmaat, & Melis, 2017). The pedagogical justification distinguishes between participation as a learning experience, and participation as an experience of actual democracy (Hoskins & Janmaat, 2019): taking part in a school council is considered as the former. This therefore appears to consider pupils primarily as *future* citizens, and addresses European Youth Goal 9 with a future outlook: school councils will address European Youth Goal 9 if participating at school increases adult participation.

Empirical research has shown a positive association between participation on school councils and adult participation in politics. The Processes Influencing Democratic Ownership and Participation (PIDOP) project (Barrett, 2012) was a multinational research project which examined predictors of political participation in nine European countries. It finds that previous high-quality experiences of political participation (including school experiences) are one of the two most reliable indicators for future participation. Similarly, Verba, Scholzman, and Brady (1995) find that previous participation in school government is one of the two most accurate predictors of adult community engagement and volunteer work. Yet the pedagogical justification does not merely hold that school and adult participation are positively associated. This might be explained by some people having a predisposition to participate at all levels (as Burns, Verba, & Schlozman, 2003, argue). Rather, it holds that participation in school *causes* increased adult participation. Indeed, Keating and Janmaat (2016) argue that participation in school activities has an independent effect on future political participation, complementing that of other drivers such as a pre-existing disposition to participate. In order to substantiate this claim, it is necessary to examine briefly the research on learning mechanisms within citizenship education to understand how this link is made.

While some argue that pupils learn by acquiring knowledge directly given to them (Anderson, Reder, & Simon, 1996), others argue that knowledge is constructed by pupils as they make sense of experience (Haste, 2004). The former has been called an acquisition model of learning (Hoskins & Janmaat, 2019). This model is exemplified by formal citizenship lessons where pupils, construed as passive receptacles for knowledge, are given information by their teachers: pupils receive an education *about* citizenship (Kerr, 1999). In the latter approach – often called constructivism – practice and activities are seen as essential for learning as pupils reconstruct their experiences in a way that is meaningful to them (Dewey, 1954). This takes place within a social context, and *inter*action is seen as an important aspect of action (Campbell, 2008; Hoskins & Janmaat, 2019). Thus 'learning is both situated and social' (Walther, 2012, p. 201). The social constructivist theory of learning has led many to suggest that the content and the pedagogy must be aligned (Kennedy, 2012). In other words, if schools wish to teach democratic participation, their learning methods must embody democratic principles (Walther, 2012; Freire, 1970; Allman, 2010). This would support education *through* citizenship (learning by participating in political activities) (Kerr, 1999; Keating & Janmaat, 2016). This approach is underpinned by the idea that action is a prerequisite of knowledge. School councils provide learning opportunities *through* citizenship in that they provide a practical and social experience of democratic processes and norms. As such, they rely on a social constructivist theory of learning.

Within the social constructivist learning approach, it is disputed exactly *how* participation in school councils increases political participation as adults. There are two main theories: learning as skills-based and theories of socialisation (Keating & Janmaat, 2016). Those who argue that it is skills-based suggest that pupils acquire certain civic competences through participatory learning experiences, and that these skills are vital for future participation. For instance, Lerner, Fisher and Weinberg (2000) highlight the so-called Five Cs, which are key developmental assets thought to be important for citizenship: competence, confidence, connection, character and compassion. Torney-Purta, Barber and Wilkenfeld (2007) highlight connection and character as particularly important amongst those for civic participation and add another – contribution – to make Six Cs. Bennet, Wells, and Freelon (2011) emphasise expression skills as important for civic participation, including the ability to communicate, negotiate and persuade. They also argue that knowledge of how democracy works is important. In the next section, we will present case studies of school councils in action. Using these, we will unpack what kinds of experiences school council members have, and how those experiences work in practice to develop the civic competences mentioned here. We will therefore return to the skills-based justification for school councils at that point and extend it by considering not just the benefits for participants, but also the implications for non-participants.

However, the skills-based justification may be an incomplete account of how school councils can promote future participation. In the social constructivist approach to learning, education is a much less controlled and precise process than the acquisition model would suggest. Because knowledge is only *indirectly* communicated from the teacher to the pupil, it has been noted that pupils often learn something from an activity which was not explicitly intended (Gear, McIntosh, & Squires, 1994): the teacher loses some control over what is learnt if the pupil is an active agent in the process. This has led some to argue that learning through citizenship is primarily a process of socialisation. Socialisation, as used here, is learning that is unconscious and unintentional on the part of the learner, and helps to inculcate the values which influence the individual's actions (Schugurensky, 2006). Because it is unconscious, it can have a subtle influence on identity formation.

Adolescence is thought to be a crucial time for political identity formation and the development of a disposition to participate (Erikson, 1968; Kahne, Crow, & Lee, 2013; Haste, 2004; Hoare, 2013). This life stage has been characterised as the "impressionable years", that is, as years in which young people are uniquely receptive to all kinds of stimuli from actors such as schools, friends, parents and the wider community in terms of how they influence their political engagement and identities (Jennings, 1979; Kinder, 2006). Moreover, recent research established that it is particularly *early* adolescence that appears to be the crucial phase for the emergence of social *inequality* in participation, as the main concern of this book. Thus, focusing on the UK context, Janmaat and Hoskins (2021) found that at the beginning of adolescence there are no social differences in political engagement but by the time children reach the age of 15 the ones from middle class backgrounds have notably higher levels of political engagement than those from disadvantaged backgrounds. After age 15 political engagement slowly rises until it reaches a plateau in the late 20s but the social difference in engagement stabilises (ibid.). These findings strongly suggest that early adolescence is the life stage to focus on when examining unequal access to school councils as one of the important influencers of political identities and engagement. Hence, we opted for 13- and 14-year-olds as research subjects (see Chapter 4, Section 1 on the ICCS 2009 data source).

What is more, activities which contribute to positive identity formation in adolescence can have an *enduring* effect. There is empirical evidence that school councils promote future participation by helping pupils develop a political identity as 'someone who takes part'. Youniss, McLellan, and Yates (1997) provide empirical evidence that participation in High School government increases the likelihood of adult voting because it helps to form the adolescent's lasting political identity as an engaged citizen with a sense of social responsibility to improve the community's wellbeing. Indeed, they find that early participation experiences are a better predictor of future engagement than socio-economic status, academic aptitude or school results. While it is perhaps the case that those from advantaged backgrounds are more likely to participate to begin with (Kam & Palmer, 2008), Youniss, McLellan, and Yates' (1997) research may indicate that participation at school can form such a strong political identity that it can override other contextual factors. This may suggest that school experiences are particularly important for pupils who would not otherwise develop a participatory political identity (Onken & Lange, 2014). From other studies (Keating & Janmaat, 2016; Torney-Purta, Barber, & Wilkenfeld, 2007), it is clear that the effects of early participation are cumulative. Thus, a snowball effect is implied, whereby early participation increases the likelihood of later participation by promoting an increasingly strong political identity (Hoskins, Janmaat, & Melis, 2017). This suggests that an increasingly bigger gap will develop over time between those who participate and those who do not. The case studies in the next section will help us to substantiate this point by identifying how exactly being a member of a school council might develop an identity conducive to future political participation. This discussion will also lay the groundwork for a discussion on the importance of equal access.

4 Contextualising School Councils within Citizenship Education

Before turning to the case studies it is useful to point out that participation in a school council is not the only pedagogical tool that has been associated with a social constructivist learning approach. It forms part of a broad family of strategies that are all characterised by participation, action, learning-by-doing, student initiative, informal and unregulated learning, and more egalitarian relationships between teachers and students. Examples of such strategies include an open climate of classroom discussions (henceforth 'open climate'), mock elections, service learning, extracurricular activities, and participation in out-of-school clubs and associations.

Open climate, as the first of these strategies, has received the bulk of the attention in the literature on citizenship education (Hahn, 1998; Torney-Purta, 2002; Campbell, 2008; Geboers et al., 2013; Knowles et al., 2018). This concept refers to a situation in which students can freely discuss political and social issues in class and are encouraged by the teacher to express their views. The teacher adopts the role of facilitator, presenting different sides to an argument and guiding the classroom discussion. At no point in this process will she impose her own views on the class and require students to embrace these views. An open climate has been argued to provide a more lively and attractive way for students to acquire knowledge about the political process and the skills to navigate it than 'dry, abstract lessons on the institutional mechanisms of the political systems' (Campbell, 2008, p. 441). Apart from enhancing political knowledge and skills, an open climate is said to foster a number of desirable affective and behavioural outcomes, such as an interest in politics, political efficacy, and political participation, through the same socialisation and identity formation processes pertaining to participation in a school council. In other words, by taking part in open discussions young people become familiar with the political process and develop a sense of engagement with and ownership of it. They come to see it as an activity for "people like me" (ibid., p. 441) and consequently develop a civic identity (Youniss et al., 1997).

Extant research has indeed found a huge amount of support for the proposed beneficial effects of open climate, irrespective of the nature of the data used (cross-sectional or longitudinal) and the methods of analyses. Thus, positive effects have been found for political participation (Torney-Purta, 2002; Hoskins et al., 2012), participatory intentions (Quintelier & Hooghe, 2013; Geboers et al., 2013), critical thinking skills (ten Dam & Volman, 2003), citizenship competences (Finkel & Ernst, 2005) and political knowledge (McDevitt & Kiousis, 2006; Campbell, 2008).

Another striking similarity with participation in a school council and with any of the other aforementioned strategies is that taking part in classroom discussions is voluntary, which means that many students can and will opt out. If the decision to take part were completely random, this non-participation would not be problematic as the ones taking part would be representative of the ones who are not. However, as a rule the choice to participate is strongly conditioned by social background with middle-class children being far more likely to engage in classroom discussions and debates than children from disadvantaged backgrounds (Kahne & Middaugh, 2008a; Hoskins et al., 2017; Hoskins & Janmaat, 2019). This means that the benefits of taking part in classroom discussions primarily accrue to children from privileged families. As these children as a rule are more politically engaged from the onset (Schlozman et al., 2012; Brady et al., 2015), an open climate may inadvertently work to *exacerbate* social inequality in political engagement. The social skew in taking part in classroom discussions is an all the more deplorable phenomenon since it has been found that children from disadvantaged backgrounds actually benefit *more* from taking part in such discussions in terms of enhancing their political engagement levels than children from middle-class backgrounds (Campbell, 2008). Thus, if participation in classroom discussions had been equal, open climate would have had the ability to *reduce* the social gap in political engagement. Since open climate has so much in common with school councils as a pedagogical strategy, the conjectures and findings regarding its social inequality mitigating and enhancing potential are highly relevant for our current study of access to school councils.

5 Case Studies

The normative and pedagogical justifications for school councils underpin our discussion of school councils in theory and elucidate the purpose(s) of school councils. We move now to an examination of school councils in practice. It is important to unpack in detail the actual experiences that school council members have, in order to see if they align with the theory. This discussion will also allow us to begin to analyse the likely consequences of differential access to school councils, by understanding what exactly participants gain from them.

We will present two case studies of school councils in Europe. These cases were selected on the basis of three considerations. First, we wanted to give examples from two different countries that are included in our data set and so form part of our analysis in the remainder of the book. This posed difficulties; in their systematic review, Mager and Nowak (2012) include relevant research published anywhere in the world in either English or German. They find that the vast majority of studies that meet their inclusion criteria were published in the UK or USA, with a small number in Ireland and a handful in other countries, such as Austria and Australia. This bias towards English-speaking countries may be due to the language of publication; we faced the same barrier to finding suitable examples in non-Anglophone Europe.

Second, we sought examples which offer enough detail to give an indication of the skills that might be developed by participation on a council. For this, we needed qualitative data describing the activities school council members engage in, in addition to quantitative data on the organisation of the council. Unfortunately, we found that research tends to be thin on such details, which limited the choice of case studies considerably.

Third, we prioritised examples of school councils involving pupils of the same age as the pupils in the ICCS dataset (14 years old). This is because some research highlights differences between older and younger members' participation on school councils. For instance, Janner-Raimondi (2015) finds evidence that the level of responsibility granted to older pupils on councils is greater. We reasoned that it would be preferable to present case studies as close in age as possible to our age group of interest.

5.1   *Case Study 1*

Keogh and Whyte (2005) present the case study of School A in an urban area of Ireland. School A is a state-funded secondary girls' school with 450 students. It is designated disadvantaged, however it serves pupils from all socio-economic backgrounds. The principal described the school council as a participative decision-making body and it is claimed that all decisions that are made at the school are automatically referred to the council for discussion (ibid., p. 104).

The school council is composed of students only. There are 36 members – known as 'prefects' – who wear badges around school to identify themselves. The Head Girl chairs the council meetings. Each class is represented by one prefect and one vice prefect. The prefects from the older year groups make up a Senior Executive Council within the main council, and positions such as secretary and treasurer are elected from the pool of the Senior Executive Council. Prefects are elected by their class members once a year. There is a round of nominations and then a secret ballot; the two pupils with the highest number of votes become members of the council. The procedures of the council, such as this election process, are decided by the council.

While teachers cannot be members of the council, adults are involved in various ways. One teacher is involved in the role of Liaison Teacher. This teacher has been in the role since she established it 20 years before. At one time, she stepped down from the role but the council 'fell apart' (Keogh & Whyte, 2005, p. 106) in her absence and so she returned. The Head Girl is elected by both staff and pupils and class teachers facilitate the student-only elections for the prefects. They prepare students for voting by leading a discussion on what sort of characteristics a prefect should have. They also count the votes for the election. Teachers are not entitled to turn up at council meetings unless invited by the council.

The full council meets once a month after school for approximately one hour and the Senior Executive Council has an additional meeting each month. It is the students on the council who decide the format of the meetings. At each meeting, there is an agreed agenda; if a prefect wants to raise an issue, she must ask in advance for it to be included on the agenda or raise it during Any Other Business at the end. Attendance and minutes are taken. The meetings are described by Keogh and Whyte (2005) as running quickly and smoothly, allowing many topics to be covered in 45 minutes. The school council is funded by profits from the vending machine (amounting to a few hundred pounds per year). This money is used for the benefit of the student body as well as charitable donations. After each council meeting, the Head Girl writes a report about the main issues raised and one copy is given to the school principal, one is put in the staff room and another is placed on the council noticeboard (which is presumably viewable by the student body, although this is not made clear).

With regard to the topics under discussion at the meetings, prefects ask their classmates in advance whether there are any issues they would like to raise, usually during an assigned lesson time. Since the prefects wear badges, students can also identify and approach them at any time to raise an issue. Keogh and Whyte (2005) provide information on changes that the council has successfully brought about at the school. Over the years, the council has made changes to the uniform; set up a photocopying system; procured bins and benches; improved the bathrooms; set up supervised study after school; and organised fundraising events. These changes are on matters that concern the pupils closely; Keogh and Whyte's report does not make clear whether other issues are raised by pupils which do not result in changes, for instance whether pupils attempt to discuss curriculum or staffing.

As for the meeting procedure, prefects are given chances to present and discuss items on the agenda. The minutes of one meeting state, 'each officer gave her report' (Keogh & Whyte, 2005, p. 134), suggesting that members have prepared in advance a report and are expected to present it coherently to the group. Keogh and Whyte state that council members do their market research and have informed discussions. This is exemplified in the meeting minutes: 'We decided that, after much research it would not be possible to have soup during lunchtime'. The 'We' also shows that council members reached a consensus as a group. To do so, prefects are likely to have listened to each other and negotiated; some will have compromised on their initial position.

Finally, in addition to the monthly meetings, council members also represent the school when there is an important visitor; when the Lord Mayor visited, it was the council members who were asked to greet him. It appears that prefects are trusted by staff to carry out privileged duties.

5.2 Case Study 2

Our second case study provides some breadth to the picture we are building of school councils in practice. The fundamental activity of a school council is to provide a decision-making forum for pupils to have their voices heard. In practice, however, there is evidence that elected members of the school council have opportunities to participate in more than just the regular council meetings. This has already been seen in the case of School A, where council members were called upon to greet the Mayor. There are many examples in the literature of school councils becoming involved in activities beyond the meetings. Specifically, these tend to be experiences that connect council members with democracy in their local communities (Whitty & Wisby, 2007a, p. 91). For instance, the European Union News (2021) reports local councillors in Wales speaking to school council members about environmental issues. School websites also report council members receiving opportunities to experience democracy that the wider student body is not offered. Council members at Barlows Primary School in Liverpool took 'a special trip to London to learn more about British rule and democracy' (Barlows Primary School, 2022); members of the Arnhem Wharf Primary School council spoke at a local council meeting and met a local MP (Arnhem Wharf Primary School, 2022). These examples serve to broaden our conception of the experiences that school council members may access. Since it appears to be common practice to employ the school council members in participatory activities beyond the usual meetings, it seems appropriate to provide a case study to illustrate what kinds of experiences these may offer.

This case study presents one school council's involvement in a participatory project in the Netherlands. School B is described as a primary school but appears to include pupils up to at least age 14 (Simovska, 2012, p. 5). School B became involved with an EU intervention project (2006–2009) called 'Shape Up'. This project aimed to promote health and wellbeing among children. The project was brought to the school by the Regional Institute for Public Health. A local facilitator and School B's headteacher decided together that Shape Up would be an aspect of the school council's work. It was thought to be within the council's remit since the project aimed to promote 'active pupil participation in influencing health determinants and school-community collaboration' (Simovska, 2012, p. 4). It is notable that this opportunity for 'active pupil participation' fell predominantly to the school council, making this experience of participation an exclusive one.

The initial stages of the Shape Up project at School B involved all pupils, who were informed about the project and took part in a survey on health-promoting changes. The results of that survey provided the basis for a whole-class discussion, from which three topics per class were selected to focus on in Shape Up. At this point, however, the class representatives (that is, members of the school council) took over, presenting their class's ideas at the city hall. The school council then worked towards two actions to promote health in their community: they aimed to improve the safety of a road near the school, and to establish a new playground for a disadvantaged community nearby.

In order to achieve these two changes, council members worked with change-makers in their local community. They prepared and submitted a request to the local authorities to reduce the speed limit on the road. They developed a detailed proposal for the new playground and presented it to city hall. Pupils also exchanged several letters with the local alderman. As in School A, the members of the council in School B acted as guides to the alderman on a visit to their school.

As for the response from the council members, the representatives were excited at the chance to communicate directly with local decision-makers. Simovska (2012) notes that there is a 'novelty to this way of working' (p. 5). This is a recognition that non-members do not experience anything akin to this. One member of the council explained that he felt nervous before going to city hall, but was able to prepare for the presentation by discussing with other council members what he should say. Simovska (2012) highlights this as an instance of peer collaboration amongst members. The pupils seemed to have a realistic outlook on the process; they were aware that the changes may not happen, but had been 'guided by adults' (p. 6) to identify and address potential barriers to change-making. In particular, the pupils were aware that the local council was likely to cite financial barriers, and prepared in advance for this eventuality by planning fundraising activities. This suggests that pupils have a good understanding of real-world barriers, as well as the resilience and competence to overcome them.

School B's headteacher believes that the council members gained a great deal through their involvement in the Shape Up project. He gives two examples. First, he refers to a female pupil of low socio-economic status (SES) whom he describes as 'very smart, very articulated' (Simovska, 2012, p. 7). Through her role as secretary on the council, she had the opportunity to help and teach other students; she used her capabilities for the benefit of others. The headteacher then refers to a 'very quiet and not very [academically] strong boy' (ibid., p. 7) who was encouraged to present at city hall during this project and surprised everyone with how confident he became. The headteacher adds, 'In this process, less resourceful pupils have a chance to get attention, to feel important, achieve something, and to build up their skills'. By 'less resourceful', the headteacher means pupils whose skills are not as developed, who may struggle academically. It is noteworthy that he believes these students in particular benefit from the experiences described during the Shape Up project at School B. If it is the case that such experiences are indeed more beneficial for 'less resourceful' students, then inequality of access becomes even more pertinent.

6 Discussion of the Case Studies

6.1 The Organisation of School Councils

In this discussion, we aim to build upon the specificity provided by the case studies and draw out common features of school councils in general. Both case studies are in line with the trend in Europe for student-only school councils. The composition of the councils – with two class representatives from each class – is also very common (Taylor & Johnson, 2002, p. 32). Structures that differ from this do exist, for instance Angell (1998) describes a class decision-making forum at a primary school which involves all pupils in the class. Keogh and Whyte (2005) provide a case study of a secondary school in Ireland where vacancies on the school council are advertised school-wide and can be filled by any suitable candidate, with only 'consideration' (p. 114) given to making sure each year group is represented. These examples are, however, the outliers, and the majority of school councils appear to involve one or two representatives from each year group or class, as in Schools A and B.

As for the selection of these representatives, School A holds elections in which only pupils get a vote. Simovska (2012) unfortunately does not provide us with detail on how representatives are selected at School B. School A's practice, though, aligns with Burnitt and Gunter's (2013) survey of 31 primary schools in England. They find that 93% of those schools with a council claim to have free (peer) elections. Taylor and Johnson (2002) also find that schools generally hold elections for council members, although note that representatives are occasionally undemocratically selected by a teacher. On the one hand, through the lens of the normative justification, it may seem obvious that elections should be held democratically: if school councils exist to respond to a need for a space for pupils to exercise their rights as citizens, then adult selection of representatives seems unacceptable. It removes pupils' autonomy and ability to self-govern, undermining the school council as a democratic space. On the other hand, viewed through the lens of the pedagogical justification, it is plausible that free elections could be damaging to the school council's project of developing an inclusive democratic society. Burnitt and Gunter (2013), for instance, query how free democratic elections will ensure diversity on the school council that is representative of the school community.

Let us consider how the democratic election system in School A could potentially lead to a lack of diversity on the school council. Keogh and Whyte (2005) explain that before the elections, class teachers lead discussions about the sorts of characteristics a prefect should have. It seems likely that these discussions would influence the pupils. By leading the discussion, the teacher has the opportunity to lead the pupils towards her image of an ideal candidate. Even if the discussion were more pupil-led, the class is nevertheless likely to come to a shared consensus on desirable characteristics through such a discussion. As for what those desirable characteristics are likely to be, there is evidence that being able to communicate with peers and listen to all views is prioritised, along with being trustworthy (Burnitt & Gunter, 2013). A discussion on which groups of pupils are likely to possess these characteristics, and therefore be overrepresented on the school council, can be found below in Chapter 3, Section 3. We note for now that the practice of electing representatives – which is by far the most common selection process – may result in a lack of diversity amongst representatives. This supposition is confirmed by our empirical analyses (Chapter 5).

6.2 *Skills and Competences*

It has already been suggested that elections may be justified on the grounds that pupils – as current citizens – have the right to choose who will represent them. In addition to this, it might be that the voting process has pedagogical advantages. By taking part in elections, the whole student body learns how to vote. Keogh and Whyte (2005) note that the pupils at School A learned how to spoil their ballot. This is an example of pupils gaining knowledge of democratic processes, one of the civic competences highlighted by Lerner, Fisher, and Weinberg (2000). It is worth noting that elections for school councils tend not to be compulsory, and Whitty and Wisby (2007a) find low engagement from the student body in elections. It is, perhaps, a shame that pupils may not take advantage of this opportunity to learn about democratic processes through the school council. On the other hand, it reflects the practice of voluntary voting in many European democratic societies. Despite evidence of a low level of engagement from the student body in elections, it remains true that elections have the potential to involve every pupil in the school.

Unfortunately, non-members' involvement outside of elections is more limited. Schools A and B seem to be fairly typical in this respect. In both cases, all pupils are involved initially in classroom discussions, but the representatives take the processes forward from that point. It will be useful to unpack the experiences the representatives have and explore how they relate to the civic competences mentioned above. The so-called Six Cs are competence, confidence, connections, character, compassion and contribution (Torney-Purta, Barber, & Wilkenfeld, 2007). The experience of representing one's peers is likely to develop participants' sense of connection, meaning positive bonds with people and institutions (Lerner, Fisher, & Weinberg, 2000). A class representative is the connecting bridge between the school as an institution and the class members as individuals. A council member must be connected to the needs of her peers and the needs of the school community. At School A, the prefects reconcile the issues raised by the student body with what is possible from the school's perspective, as seen in the decision on lunchtime soup.

Council members have opportunities to develop compassion, meaning empathy and a sense of social justice (Lerner, Fisher, & Weinberg, 2000). At School B, this is exemplified by the female pupil of low SES who used her position on the council to help others. At School A, the council members decide to spend some of the budget on charitable donations and organise fundraising events, demonstrating a sense of social justice.

Speaking in public forums could develop pupils' confidence. The headteacher at School B believed that this was the case, especially for 'less resourceful' students; the boy who had been overlooked in the classroom found that he could thrive in a different environment (Simovska, 2012). Lerner, Fisher and Weinberg (2000) also link confidence to a feeling of self-efficacy; experiences of success in new or uncomfortable situations are likely to develop this. This suggests that bringing about real change may increase feelings of self-efficacy and confidence, leading to greater participation later in life. The council members in School B had the opportunity to make meaningful changes in their community. In doing so, they also learned about real-world democratic processes, from writing letters to decision-makers to recognising financial barriers to change. Learning how to navigate this process, and experiencing success in doing so, may have increased the pupils' confidence that they can achieve change in their community.

The council meetings at School A are run efficiently: prefects take attendance and minutes, and much is reportedly achieved in 45 minutes. This demonstrates the first of the 6 Cs: competence, that is, the ability to operate effectively. Expression skills of the kind that Bennet, Wells, and Freelon (2011) emphasise are also evident at the meetings. In order to reach a consensus on the issue of soup, the prefects have to communicate, negotiate and persuade. This aligns with Ferreira, Azevedo and Menezes' (2012) finding that pupils who take part in councils develop their communication skills, leading to better conflict resolution skills.

While council meetings tend to call for oral communication skills, there is evidence that written communication skills may also be developed by participating on the school council. The Head Girl at School A writes a report after each meeting, and at School B they wrote letters to the alderman. In his case study of a UK primary school, Cotmore (2004) reports that school council members communicate with the student body by writing letters to individuals who have raised an issue via the council's suggestion box. There is, therefore, evidence that communication is a key skill for school council members. Whether the council members are already competent and possess good communication skills, or the experience of participating helps to develop these skills, is unclear from the case studies. In Chapter 6, Section 5, we argue that it is likely to be both.

6.3 *Political Identity*

So far, we have explored the skills and competences that school councils are thought to develop. Our discussion in Chapter 2, Section 3 highlighted an alternative theoretical outcome of school councils: the formation of a political identity. That is, the development of pupils' self-concept as someone who takes part in such things. The case studies provide us with some idea of how a political identity might be formed by participation on the school council. At School A, the pupils wear badges to show that they are prefects. This seems to be a common practice, found in many case studies (Whitty & Wisby, 2007a; Taylor & Johnson, 2002). A badge is a visible marker, making council members identifiable to peers and teachers. It may create a feeling of exclusivity around the council, since only some pupils are entitled to wear the badge. Wearing a badge may therefore reinforce a member's own identity as someone who participates. In addition to badges, the political identity of school council representatives may be reinforced by their experiences of brushing shoulders with those in power, such as the Mayor or local MP. These experiences may promote a sense of familiarity and belonging in politics. In contrast, those pupils who do not have these opportunities may feel that there is distance between them and real-world politics.

Cotmore's (2004) case study of a primary school in England provides a useful insight into the question of identity on the council. One teacher interviewed noted a sense of 'difference' (ibid., p. 62) for the representatives compared with other pupils. As one school council member puts it, being a councillor 'gives you more freedom' (ibid.). The teacher captures the ambiguity of her role in the council: 'It's most definitely not teaching [...] But it's definitely not not teaching' (ibid.). The ambiguity in the teacher-pupil relationship during council meetings may reinforce the identity of council members as special: they have access to an exclusive relationship with teachers and freedom in school which non-members do not.

6.4 Criticisms of School Councils and a Response

The discussion above has emphasised the benefits that school councils are thought to bring to representatives. We recognise, however, that there is a debate in the literature on how beneficial they really are. One point of contention is the extent to which school councils enact real change (e.g. Cross, Hulme, & McKinney, 2014; Alderson, 2000; Bennett, 2012). Some research finds that school councils tend to effect change only in areas that don't challenge the authoritarian structures of school. This charge has been levelled against school councils across Europe, with recent literature finding the same as literature from the early 2000s. For instance, Haraldstad, Tveit, and Kovač's (2022) study on democracy in four Norwegian lower secondary schools finds that school councils have 'a materialistic orientation' (p. 82); their remit is limited to material improvements. Whitty and Wisby (2007a) find that common topics under discussion include facilities, lunches and uniforms. At the 31 schools surveyed by Burnitt and Gunter (2013), only 23% of the school councils regularly engage in long-term strategic planning for the school, for instance by planning for the next year. School A's list of achievements, too, seems limited to material improvements for the student body, rather than curriculum or engagement with school strategy. This observation may make one suspicious of the principal's claim that *all* decisions at School A are automatically referred to the council. We therefore recognise that the decision-making power of school councils is contested. Especially with regard to the output and achievements of councils, we agree that their scope may be somewhat limited.

With regard to the quality of participation, the picture is also ambiguous. It is interesting that the council at School A 'fell apart' when the liaison teacher stepped down. This suggests reliance on the teacher, at odds with the apparent independence with which the council is organised by the prefects. One is left wondering whether representatives are genuinely leading the school council, or whether the school council is an adult-led arena in which the pupils are invited to participate (Hart, 1992). In contrast to School A, Cotmore's (2004) case study provides examples of the destabilisation of the usual adult-child dynamic in council meetings. The authority of the teacher appears softened and at times inverted so that the child has authority. For example, in one meeting, the teacher chairing the meeting makes a suggestion regarding the frequency of council meetings, and a pupil challenges it. The teacher goes with the pupil's suggestion instead. This suggests that, while the teacher may have guided the meeting, she was willing to defer to pupils on decision-making. This corresponds with rung six of Hart's ladder of participation: the council is adult-initiated, but pupils hold decision-making power. It appears that the quality of participation on school councils can vary, but that there are likely to be some examples that correspond to Hart's higher rungs.

Yet, the debate does not end there. Some have questioned more radically whether education – even at its most effective – can have an effect on political participation at all. Kam and Palmer (2008), for instance, contend that the effect of education is merely a proxy for social background. They claim that those from advantaged backgrounds are more likely to participate and to find these experiences fruitful than their disadvantaged peers, and that this explains the empirical link between participation experiences in education and adult participation. If true, this may undermine the pedagogical justification for school councils. However, Kam and Palmer have merely investigated the effect of college education and have not looked more specifically at the effect of taking part in a school council. Of course, pupils from disadvantaged backgrounds are likely to be underrepresented in school councils (which we will indeed show to be the case later on), but if participation in such councils does have an independent effect on future participation, as claimed by Keating and Janmaat (2016) and noted earlier, then there is every reason to value such councils and to step up efforts to increase the participation of low SES pupils in them. Moreover, such councils can still be justified as important on normative grounds. Thus, going forward, we acknowledge the debate around the efficacy of school councils as learning measures, but suggest that this does not fully undermine their worth in addressing European Youth Goal 9.

7 Why School Councils?

Having explored in detail the theoretical basis for school councils as well as their practical functioning, we can draw out some reasons for our focus on school councils in this book, in preference to those other pedagogical tools mentioned, such as open climate. First, school councils are a particularly powerful version of participatory learning because they involve pupils having an impact and making change. Other participatory learning experiences may not involve actual change (think, for example, of mock elections). The second reason is a methodological one. Participation and non-participation are clear measures (though we recognise that the quality and kind of this participation may vary). This is in contrast to open climate, which is difficult to quantify and relies on subjective experience and perceptions. The data collected by the ICCS survey on school council participation lends itself to the statistical analyses we carry out. Our third – and most important – reason concerns the potential for inequality to arise in school councils. Because school councils almost always involve representatives, by their nature they are exclusive. Thus, the question of access becomes particularly pertinent.

8   Chapter Summary

In this chapter, we have surveyed the existing literature on school councils, drawing out how they work in theory and in practice. With regard to the theory, we identified two ways that they might be thought to address the goal of providing space and participation to all. On the one hand, the normative justification responds to this goal in the present, considering pupils as current citizens who have a right to democratic participation opportunities. On the other hand, the pedagogical justification looks to the future, justifying school councils on the basis that they have the potential to increase future political participation by developing the skills and/or identity needed for engagement. As for the practices of school councils, we identified the common organisational structures of school councils, along with what experiences they offer pupils. We related these experiences to the competences and identities they are likely to develop in those who participate. We recognise concerns over the quality of some school councils; however, it is beyond the scope of this book to explore this body of literature in more depth. For the purposes of this study, it is enough to have established that, from both a normative and pedagogical perspective, school councils have the potential to meet European Youth Goal 9.

Yet it is not for all students that school councils may meet European Youth Goal 9. On the contrary, our analysis found that the structure of school councils is such that it is the representatives who reap the benefits of participation. The rest of the student body remains largely uninvolved. This is especially pertinent given that the value of what school councils achieve is so contested. Since school councils may not have the power to implement changes for the good of all, the benefits of a school council lie in the experience of participating. Therefore, with previous research that has pointed to this issue (Whitty & Wisby, 2007a; Wyness, 2009), we turn to the main topic of this book: access to school councils. Which pupils, in which countries and schools, and with what characteristics, have the opportunity to be a representative on the school council?

CHAPTER 3

Questions of Access

The question of access is relevant to school councils because it is a non-compulsory learning activity (Hoskins, Janmaat, & Melis, 2017): schools throughout the EU generally have a choice as to whether or not to have a school council, and most school councils involve only some pupils at the school. This has led some to see school councils as exclusive clubs (Whitty & Wisby, 2007b). Some pupils (from some countries, schools and backgrounds) may be accessing the opportunities afforded by school councils more than others. This should be of concern to anyone concerned with equality and youth political participation. The literature suggests that school councils do, at least potentially, address European Youth Goal 9. Yet if there is unequal access, then school councils are not providing opportunities for space and participation for *all*, both in the present and in the future. In this section, we will explore the literature on access to political participation opportunities at three levels: national, school and individual. We will highlight some theoretical barriers to pupils participating in school councils. Since the literature on access to school councils is extremely limited, we will engage mainly with the literature on youth political participation in general and make links between this and councils.

1 National Level

Recently, there have been calls to consider variation in citizenship education between national contexts (Kerr, 1999; Youniss & Yates, 1999; Haste, 2004; Klingemann, Fuchs, & Zielonka, 2006; Kitanova, 2019). Cross-national variation in citizenship education has been noted; it is thought that different political institutions, histories and ideologies have an important impact on this variation (Kerr, 1999; Han et al., 2013). This is particularly pertinent in the context of Europe, where supranational goals for education are increasingly set by the EU, yet states are often allowed flexibility in how they meet these goals (Keating, 2014). This raises the question: Is European Youth Goal 9 being addressed in a similar and equitable way across Europe? There has been some research into how different versions of democracies may shape pupils' experiences of democratic education, as well as their subsequent participation as adults. In grouping similar countries, some have emphasised the relevance of the former communist nations' recent democratisation (Flanagan, Beyers, & Žukauskienė,

2012; Youniss & Yates, 1999; Haste, 2004) while others have made distinctions between western and northern European nations (Klemenčič, 2012; Helgøy & Homme, 2006). In this section, we will explore how the concept of *political culture* has been used to highlight differences between conceptions of citizenship and participation in Europe. We will draw out different norms regarding public voice in decision-making (Klingemann, Fuchs, & Zielonka, 2006). From this, we will develop our hypothesis regarding pupils' access to school councils in different EU nations.

Under the broad umbrella of 'democracy', there can exist a variety of political cultures. The political culture of a country is created by the political convictions, ideologies, behaviours and attitudes of its citizens (Almond & Verba, 1963). As such, it is tied to certain norms: different societies have different expectations of citizenship, including different conceptions of what is required of citizens and the state (Preuss et al., 2003; Janmaat & Green, 2022). This distinction between different democratic political cultures is useful to apply in the field of education; fundamentally, it characterises the relationship between formal governance (the education institution) and public voice (the student body).

The political culture in the Nordic countries tends to be characterised by notions of equality, inclusivity and widespread participation (Wilensky, 2002; Green, Janmaat, & Han, 2009). Wilensky (2002) describes these countries as neo-corporatist, which refers to the way in which they organise interest groups (that is, informal organisations that have a political interest). In neo-corporatist countries, interest groups are invited into policy-making processes and actively supported by the government. For instance, in Sweden, government funding is given to those who may not otherwise organise themselves effectively, such as refugees (Adan, 2018, p. 12). This indicates a political culture in which there exists a norm that all people will be consulted in decision-making processes (Helgøy & Homme, 2006). Walther (2012) finds that this political culture is reflected in the education system in the Nordic countries, where pupils enjoy a 'pronounced status as co-citizens' (p. 194). In such a political culture, one would surely expect many opportunities for pupil voice and representation within school and, therefore, a high proportion of schools with school councils.

While the literature largely converges on its description of the political culture in the Nordic countries, there is some conflict concerning theories of political cultures in western Europe. Wilensky (2002) and Green, Janmaat and Han (2009) all emphasise the Liberal culture of the UK and Ireland. In such a culture, there is an emphasis on choice, individual rights and opportunities. On the one hand, Wilensky suggests that this means it is a least-corporatist democracy, where competition between interest groups is allowed to flourish. This is thought to undermine principles of equality between different groups in decision-making processes and implies less concern with fair representation. Such a conception of the political culture in the UK and Ireland may imply that opportunities to participate on a school council are limited, as there is less concern with giving under-represented or powerless groups (such as children) a platform. On the other hand, Green, Janmaat and Han (2009) suggest that the liberal political culture in these countries engenders increased levels of public participation in decision-making, as citizens are thought to be entitled to a platform to express their opinions and change things to their liking. This understanding of the liberal political culture would predict more opportunities to participate on a school council, as it may be argued pupils have a right to a say in their education.

With regard to the Mediterranean countries, the literature could again be used to justify two contrasting predictions regarding levels of school council access. Green, Janmaat, and Han (2009) and Janmaat and Green (2022) characterise the political culture in these countries as Republican. In such a culture, the state is considered primary but, importantly, composed of individuals, who have a duty to participate in politics. In this way, individuals are thought to create the state, for the common good, through collective deliberation. It may be that Republicanism is therefore linked to more widespread access to school councils as participation in decision-making is seen as a duty, not a choice. Yet Walther (2012) identifies a paternalistic approach towards young people in the Mediterranean countries, involving a structural deficit in youth empowerment policies. This would predict fewer opportunities for pupil participation in these countries.

Drawing on Esping Andersen's (1990) classification of welfare regimes, Green, Janmaat, and Han (2009) characterise the political culture of Austria, Germany and the low countries as conservative. In this political culture, society is conceived of as a stable and enduring social hierarchy, where citizens are bound together by tradition. There is much less emphasis placed on individual rights, liberties and equality, as citizens are expected to show deference to the established social order. This conception of citizenship would surely predict fewer opportunities to participate on school councils, as individual voice and inclusive participation are seen as less important.

Turning now to eastern Europe, the political culture in eastern countries is sometimes distinguished from western Europe based on the *age* of democracy. Kitanova (2019) argues that the democratic history of a country can cause differences in youth participation between EU countries. She suggests that more advanced democracies have stronger norms of participation and more opportunities to participate. In her paper, democracies established before 1988 are considered 'advanced', and ex-communist countries, with democracies established post-1988, are considered 'new'. Fuchs and Klingemann's (2006) empirical study finds that the political culture becomes gradually less democratic (measured by support for democratic values like the rule of law) as one looks east in Europe. This conceptualisation of political culture would predict fewer opportunities for youth participation in eastern Europe, while older democracies might be expected to have more opportunities, including more school councils.

Based on the preceding discussion, we suggest the following hypothesis:

Hypothesis 1: The Nordic democracies will have more opportunities for participation on a school council, while eastern European and Conservative countries will have fewer opportunities.

With regards to the Mediterranean and Liberal cultures, the conflicting theories suggest that this should be analysed through empirical data. We therefore refrain from formulating a hypothesis at this point, but will investigate the proportion of schools in each political culture which have a school council in Chapter 5, Section 2. This will perhaps show which theory is better justified by the data.

The preceding discussion has focused on the predicted aggregate, school-level patterns of school council access. However, on the basis of political culture, it may also be possible to predict patterns of individual-level access to councils. That is, it may be that in certain political cultures, there is more equality regarding which people, from which backgrounds, access political opportunities, both in school and in society. Hoskins and Janmaat (2019) find that the strength of the relation between an individual's socio-economic status (SES) and their intention to vote varies enormously throughout Europe. In particular, they identify the UK as the country in which there is the strongest positive association between SES and voting intention (ibid., p. 2). This may be explained by the UK's Liberal political culture, which emphasises competition over equality. It might be supposed that countries with a Liberal political culture have greater inequality of access between individuals, based on socio-demographic characteristics such as SES. Conversely, it may be that political cultures that emphasise equality of representation have more even and equitable access to school councils between individuals with diverse socio-demographic characteristics. We therefore suggest the following hypothesis concerning individuals' access to councils in different political cultures.

Hypothesis 2: The effect of individuals' socio-demographic characteristics on school council participation is smaller in the Nordic countries and larger in the Liberal countries.

2   School Level

In order to illustrate the potential differences in opportunities found at the school level in Europe, we will begin with the extreme example of Singapore. The citizenship education in Singapore is unique in that it is explicitly differentiated between different school tracks (Ho, 2012). That is, pupils with different levels of academic attainment are educated for different *kinds* of citizenship. While those on the higher track are taught the skills and knowledge needed to be critical thinkers and leaders, those on the lower track are given just the knowledge needed to follow the state dutifully (ibid.). Interestingly, the future leaders and thinkers are given more opportunities for discussion, governance and participation in political activities, which surely corresponds to education *through* citizenship. The example of Singapore illustrates Amnå's (2012) assertion that schools have the potential to empower their pupils politically, or to merely tame and discipline them. It appears that Singapore has embraced this split potential. However, this surely leads to political inequalities, in that some children are given the skills needed to lead or influence government and others are left largely voiceless. Indeed, the gap lies not only in the skills gap, but more fundamentally in the difference in their conceptions of citizenship (Ho, 2012).

The idea that schools should differentiate not only the academic curriculum but also the citizenship curriculum is deeply objectionable to a western public. American researchers take it as given that political equality is essential, yet there is evidence that unacceptable civic inequalities are being reinforced by the education system (Verba, 2003; Kahne & Middaugh, 2008a). There is a growing body of evidence that schools have the power to hinder or encourage the development of engaged civic identities (Rubin, 2007; Eckstein, Noack, & Gniewosz, 2012) but that the political socialisation of pupils varies between school types as they promote different political identities, as in Singapore (Kahne & Middaugh, 2008a; Amnå, 2012; Westheimer & Kahne, 2004). In the European context, the principle of political equality has also been upheld by researchers (e.g. van de Werfhorst, 2009) but there has not been the same systematic research into how schools might reproduce political inequalities by promoting different kinds of citizenship. In this section, we will explore the existing literature on this topic, from Europe and elsewhere, to investigate whether it is likely that different school types are providing different levels of support for European Youth Goal 9.

The role and impact of elite education on reproducing social inequalities has been researched in some detail (Aggleton & Maxwell, 2016). Khan (2011) has shed some light on how elite education institutions (in his study, a private school in the USA) socialise pupils into a certain way of being in the world and relating to others which is advantageous to them: he finds that pupils at elite institutions develop a sense of self-efficacy and ability to move up a hierarchy. Khan suggests that this leads to an unequal democracy, in which elite pupils are better able to participate in political life. Kennedy and Power (2008) make a similar observation about elite private schools in Ireland, while Ichilov (2002) confirms this finding in Israel. It would appear, then, that van de Werfhorst's (2009) claim that different secondary school types focus on the enhancement of different social competences is justified in many contexts. Whitty and Wisby (2007b) provide some evidence that school councils can play a part in this differential learning. They find that private schools give pupils more genuine power and responsibility to improve their schools through school councils than state schools do. This would suggest that private schools are providing better opportunities for pupils to develop leadership and participation skills. This is evidence of *qualitative* differences in school councils between private and public schools; Whitty and Wisby do not mention *quantitative* differences, which is the topic of the current study. However, it seems reasonable to hypothesise that private schools provide more, as well as better, opportunities to develop the skills and/or identity necessary for political participation. Given that school councils are thought to develop these skills, we suggest the following hypothesis:

Hypothesis 3: Private schools are more likely to have a school council than public schools.

Yet across Europe, the private school criterion is not always contextually relevant. Some countries, such as England, have a long tradition of elite, private schooling (Reay, 2006), while others, such as Scandinavia, do not (Helgøy & Homme, 2006). Instead, the social composition of a school may better capture socio-economic segregation in the education system. Flemmen (2016) finds segregation on the basis of social background across Europe, even in relatively egalitarian education systems, such as in Scandinavia. There is some evidence that schools with many socially disadvantaged students use different pedagogical approaches to schools with an advantaged student body (Bowles & Gintis, 1976). In particular, they may focus more narrowly on academic attainment with less 'latitude for a broad curriculum' (Bischoff, 2016, p. 100). In addition, they may emphasise rote learning above critical thinking skills and free choice (Hoskins & Janmaat, 2019). Michaela school in north London has faced criticism on this front; some have argued that its strict teaching methods may narrow opportunities for free and critical thinking (Adams, 2016; Abrams, 2017).

It may be that schools with more disadvantaged pupils face increased pressure to raise attainment, but this may come at the expense of other experiences (Castagno, 2008). McFarland and Starmanns (2009) provide evidence that uneven access to school councils may be a manifestation of these pedagogical and structural differences between schools with different socio-economic compositions. In the context of the USA, they find that school councils vary in both quality and quantity between schools with different SES compositions: schools with many disadvantaged pupils tend to lack school councils or have merely tokenistic councils. This may be because school councils promote the active participation of students, which may not be a priority in such schools. We therefore hypothesise the following:

Hypothesis 4: Schools with a high proportion of low SES pupils are less likely to have a school council than schools with a high SES composition.

There is also evidence that the ethnic composition of a school may influence opportunities relevant to political participation. In the USA, Mowen and Parker (2017) have noted a positive association between the proportion of black pupils at a school and security measures. Their research is grounded in the theory that school authorities feel threatened by large minority ethnic groups, leading to harsher discipline measures. It is plausible that a high proportion of ethnic minority pupils in a school may be linked to other authoritarian measures including less emphasis on democratic principles and fewer opportunities for pupil voice. McFarland and Starmanns (2009) present empirical evidence to support this theory, finding that schools with a high proportion of ethnic minority students are less likely to have a school council because of an over-emphasis on discipline. In addition, Campbell (2007) highlights research which suggests ethnic homogeneity within a classroom leads to increased political engagement because staff feel able to permit and even facilitate open discussion of controversial topics in the knowledge that conflict will most likely be avoided. This author finds through his own empirical research that ethnic diversity in the classroom leads to fewer opportunities for political discussion, which in turn diminishes pupils' intentions to participate in the future. Based on this literature, we have formulated the following hypothesis.

Hypothesis 5: Schools with a high proportion of ethnic minority pupils are less likely to have a school council.

On the basis of this literature on school type, there is a clear need for empirical research into whether a Singapore-style differentiation of citizenship education between different types of schools exists in the EU. If we find uneven access to school councils, this would be evidence that pupils at only *some* schools are being given space and participation opportunities and this may be reproducing political inequalities.

3 Individual Level

At the individual level, we are considering barriers to political participation from the developmental perspective (Youniss, McLellan, & Yates, 1997). This construes barriers to participation from the perspective of the development of the person, rather than by reference to external, structural barriers (see Henn & Foard, 2014, for an example of the latter). Youniss, McLellan, and Yates (1997) focus on the political socialisation of the child and their subsequent identity formation. They contend that identity is key to engagement, and that disengaged political identities can therefore be a barrier to participation. An alternative and enlightening developmental perspective can also be found in capability theory (McCowan & Unterhalter, 2013). This theory considers the capability individuals have to convert received opportunities and resources into power and influence (Sen, 1980; Nussbaum, 2000). For example, a citizen's ability to influence decisions will depend partly on her own capacities for communication and construction of argument. It is argued that citizens will have these competences to differing extents, depending on their circumstances. Barriers to participation thus include a lack of the competences, knowledge and skills needed to participate (Amnå, 2012). Both of these developmental perspectives show the inadequacy of equality of opportunity: if differences in participation are a product of personal attributes, then the mere availability of opportunities will not address the barriers. Rather, political equality will depend on recognising heterogeneity in citizens (McCowan & Unterhalter, 2013); people will need different amounts of support to participate equally. The fact that school councils may be open to everyone does not, therefore, mean that everyone is equally able to participate.

The structure of school councils tends to be such that prior developmental experience is likely to cause unequal access (Hoskins & Janmaat, 2019). A vicious circle is identified by Walther (2012), who argues that youth participation, including on school councils, appears to follow the rule, 'first learn, then participate' (p. 190). This implies that only those who already have the necessary skills are able to participate in school councils. Burnitt and Gunter (2013) find that the diversity of pupils on school councils is seriously limited by the requirement for good communication skills. If this is the case, this would undermine councils in their capacity both as democratic forums and as learning tools. The literature highlights two ways in which school councils may be particularly vulnerable to this problem. First, because it tends to be voluntary, it may be that only certain children put themselves forward for roles. This may mean that individuals are 'unknowingly complicit' (Hoskins & Janmaat, 2019, p. 56) in perpetuating inequalities. In this view, barriers at the individual level are importantly different from those at the national and the school level, where inequalities are due to external constraints on individuals, imposed by those in charge. Second, the election process may reflect teachers' and pupils' preconceptions regarding who would be a good candidate. This was seen in case study 1, where the class teachers were asked to lead a discussion with their classes before elections to identify appropriate characteristics for a representative. This can turn elections into little more than popularity contests based on who appears to already have the identity and competences that are desirable for the role (Taylor & Johnson, 2002; Bennett, 2012). Thus there may be unequal access to school councils because they involve a selection process.

Focusing now on particular groups, the question of access can be reframed to consider which groups, and why, are likely to lack the capabilities and identity needed for selection on school councils. Beyond the school context, young people do not all participate in politics in a uniform way and the PIDOP report (Barrett, 2012) provides compelling evidence that there are *patterns* in political participation amongst different groups, which suggests systematic inequality. Where certain contexts tend towards reduced participation, it has been termed *political disadvantage* (Levinson, 2007). Kahne and Middaugh (2008b) highlight the need to consider how schools might be exacerbating the political disadvantage of individuals with certain socio-demographic characteristics by providing them with fewer civic learning opportunities. We will, therefore, explore some of the theoretical explanations found in the literature for why some groups are associated with different levels of political engagement. The empirical research that follows will test whether these same groups also have reduced access to school councils. If certain capabilities and identities are prerequisites for participation on school councils, then it seems likely that they will.

Low socio-economic status (SES) appears to be linked to low political participation partly via social (or cultural) capital. Hoskins and Janmaat (2019) highlight that children obtain different kinds of capital depending on their upbringing in different social milieus. Middle-class children tend to acquire the type of social capital that is rewarded by schools. Especially pertinent for school councils, they may also acquire the competences needed for deliberation and compromise, for example through frequent discussions about the world and politics (ibid.). Pupils of low SES may have fewer opportunities to engage in such discussions. This means that children may enter school on an 'uneven playing field' (ibid., p. 49): pupils of high SES are perhaps more likely to have the capabilities and civic competences needed to participate on a school council. Some empirical research indicates that this potential for uneven political participation is indeed realised at school. Hoskins, Janmaat and Melis (2017) find that low SES is associated with reduced access to voluntary political activities in schools. Whitty and Wisby's (2007b) qualitative study gives some indication that socio-economically advantaged pupils are over-represented on school councils. However, they call for more quantitative research on the link between social background and participation on councils; the current study addresses this gap in the literature.

Hypothesis 6: Pupils of low SES are less likely to participate on school councils.

While there is evidence that SES has a direct effect on the skills needed for political engagement in the way described above, other research points to a more complex relationship between SES and political engagement, which is determined by the social environment. Nie, Junn, and Stehlik-Barry (1996) argue that the social environment is important in explaining engagement patterns for political activities that are competitive in nature. These authors contend that SES should be understood as relative to other people, rather than absolute. In other words, an individual's SES depends on the SES of those around him/her. This understanding of SES is used to argue that education has a positional effect on political engagement: education is seen as a factor that helps to sort people into a hierarchy of SES, and then those with relatively higher SES are thought to be more engaged in competitive political activities because they are likely to have more success (Campbell, 2006). The work of Nie, Junn and Stehlik-Barry is relevant to school councils for two reasons. First, these authors demonstrate that this understanding of SES is particularly pertinent for competitive political activities, of which a school council is a good example: it is a zero-sum game because for someone to be a representative, someone else is prevented from being so. Second, it suggests that the effect of an individual's SES on political engagement may depend on the social (school) environment. Specifically, a student with average SES in the sample size at large would be expected to participate less in a school where those around him/her were of higher SES (Campbell, 2006). We therefore suggest the following hypothesis:

Hypothesis 7: The effect of an individual's SES is positional, such that a pupil of average SES participates less at a school of high SES composition.

SES may also be the cause of the indirect link between high educational attainment and aspirations and increased political engagement (Onken & Lange, 2014). The theoretical mechanism is that families of high SES tend to encourage high educational aspirations *and* political participation (ibid.). Thus social origins are the initial cause, from which stems engagement with both formal education and politics, creating a positive correlation between educational attainment, aspirations and political engagement. This mechanism does not, however, preclude the possibility that schools can disrupt this process. Just as schools are thought to be able to raise the educational attainment of pupils of low SES, so too are they thought to be able to increase their political engagement (Hoskins & Janmaat, 2019). Unfortunately, there is evidence that schools are currently *not* disrupting this link. In their study of Californian high school students, Kahne and Middaugh (2008b) find a positive correlation between educational aspirations and access to political learning opportunities at school. To our knowledge, there is not yet a body of literature on whether this is the case in Europe, as well.

Hypothesis 8: Pupils with low educational aspirations are less likely to participate on school councils.

The relationship between ethnicity and political participation is complex, with generalising statements failing to capture the diversity that exists. There is diversity in how minority groups engage with politics and also levels of engagement. Equally, there are differences in political participation both between and within minority groups in England (Heath et al., 2013). Uberoi and Johnston (2021) found that people from an ethnic minority are generally less likely to vote than white people in the UK. However, the same report found that minority ethnic groups seem to be more engaged than white groups and have more interest in getting involved in politics (ibid.). There is evidence that the picture across Europe may be similar. The European Network Against Racism's (2019) analysis following the 2019 European Parliament elections found that national ethnic minority groups were hugely underrepresented. The Council of Europe (2016) also reports that ethnic minority groups are underrepresented in European governments and institutions. Sandovici and Listhaug (2010), however, find that it is only when it comes to *voting* that there are significant differences between the political participation levels of ethnic minority and majority groups in Europe. On a measure of political participation that excludes voting but includes other political activities (such as contacting politicians, signing a petition, and taking part in protests) these authors find that ethnic minority groups participate at similar rates to the majority population.

The question of how this picture is reflected in schools is unclear in the case of Europe. Evidence does, however, exist on this topic for the USA. It is therefore useful to touch briefly on patterns of ethnic minority participation in the USA. In the USA, the evidence suggests that ethnic minority groups have lower levels of participation in politics than the white ethnic majority (US Census Bureau, 2021; Fraga, 2018). This has been explained in various ways. Burns, Verba, and Schlozman (2003) contend that participatory differences between ethnic groups can be largely explained by differences in SES. They suggest that ethnic minority groups in the USA are often of lower SES, and thus the mechanism leading to lower engagement of lower SES groups described above can explain the influence of ethnicity on participation. Others have highlighted the importance of identity in the participation of ethnic minorities. Torney-Purta, Barber, and Wilkenfeld (2007) suggest that Latino youths in the USA tend to be less politically engaged than their white peers because their parents tend to be less politically engaged. Haste (2004) argues that children naturally identify with their family and others who are like them. It is thus possible that Latino teenagers may be socialised to include political *dis*engagement as part of their Latino identity. Barreto's (2010) research on Latino voters in the USA supports this supposition; he finds that ethnic identification with politicians is an important motivator for voters, while a lack of identification discourages engagement.

Turning now to how this pattern is manifested in schools, Kahne and Middaugh (2008b) have found exclusion of ethnic minorities from politics reflected in American schools: they find that African Americans and Latinos are less likely to have access to learning through political activities at school than their peers. Levinson (2007) has also found evidence of evidence of a civic achievement gap in the USA between ethnic minority groups and white groups.

Since the political engagement of ethnic minority groups in Europe seems to be more mixed, it is important to investigate the effect of ethnicity on participation on school councils to find out whether the findings about the USA education system apply equally to European education. Our hypothesis (below) is based on the patterns found in the USA. Torney-Purta, Barber, and Wilkenfeld (2007) call for quantitative research into inequalities between ethnic groups in Europe using large and representative samples of students, across many schools and contexts. The ICCS 2009 dataset will allow us to do this.

Hypothesis 9: Pupils from a minority ethnic background are less likely to participate on school councils.

Explaining the political disadvantage of ethnic minority individuals by linking ethnicity to SES – as Burns, Verba, and Schlozman (2003) do – indicates that these two factors may not be completely independent in how they affect political engagement. If ethnic minority students are less likely to participate because they tend to be of lower SES, it seems that ethnic minority pupils of high SES may have different patterns of engagement. The PIDOP report also provides evidence that SES and ethnicity interact to produce varied and compound effects (Barrett, 2012). Hoskins and Janmaat (2019) call for more research into how the intersections of socio-demographic characteristics might contribute to political inequalities. We will address this by testing the following hypothesis:

Hypothesis 10: The effect of an individual's ethnicity on school council participation will depend on his/her SES.

There is a need to explore the impact of ethnicity in the school environment specifically. Youdell (2003) understands institutional racism in UK schools as stemming from the interaction between the school's construction of a desirable learner identity and students' racial identities. The desirable learner identity is often classed, gendered and raced (Gillborn, 1990), with students that do not conform to the ideal perceived as inappropriate or lesser. It may be that ethnic minority students, then, are marginalised by school culture. In other words, it may be that an individual's ethnicity interacts with the school's social environment to produce varying effects. It seems plausible that a school with mainly ethnic majority pupils may have a narrower definition of the ideal learner, and ethnic minority students might more easily be cast as deviating from that norm. Given the election process for school councils, in which the ideal candidate is likely to be selected by peers and staff, it may be that ethnic minority students have different levels of access to school councils depending on the ethnic composition – and thus norms – of the school environment. We therefore suggest the following hypothesis:

Hypothesis 11: The greater the proportion of ethnic majority pupils, the stronger the effect of ethnic identity.

Differences in participation experiences at school have also been noted between genders. The differences tend to be regarding the *type* of participation, rather than the frequency (Eckstein, Noack, & Gniewosz, 2012), which distinguishes gender from the other characteristics discussed. At school, Hoskins and Janmaat (2019) find that girls appear to have more access to formal citizenship education and a more open classroom environment than boys. They speculate that this may be because teachers respond to girls' behaviour which they perceive as less aggressive. This hypothesis implies that the learnt behaviour traits of pupils (such as level of aggressivity) may influence the opportunities they have access to. McCowan and Unterhalter (2013) support this theory with their claim that boys and girls may be exposed to different socialisation experiences, leading to variations in capabilities and identities. Contrary to this theory, Taylor and Johnson (2002) find that school councils in England tend to have a fairly equal gender balance in practice. Their report suggests that the selection process can enforce gender equality more easily than other kinds of equality: many schools are found to stipulate one female and one male representative per class. It is therefore necessary to explore further how gender may impact on access to school councils, while bearing in mind that apparent gender equality on councils may be the result of a formal requirement.

Hypothesis 12: Neither girls nor boys are more likely to participate on school councils.

In summary, this section has highlighted a developmental approach to understanding the political disadvantage of some individuals. If schools are microcosms of society, it is plausible that they reflect the same barriers to participation found in society: pupils who do not have the prerequisite identities and competences may be excluded from participation spaces such as school councils. If schools fail to provide space for participation for all individuals in the present, they are not only potentially denying some pupils their rights now, but also in the future by failing to develop the identities and competences needed for adult participation. It is thus of paramount importance to understand whether all groups have equal access to school councils and, in so doing, address the research gap on this topic indicated by many authors.

CHAPTER 4

A Quantitative Approach

1   Data Source

Our data source is the International Civic and Citizenship Education Study (ICCS) (2009), which is a study conducted by the International Association for the Evaluation of Educational Achievement (IEA). It is an international study, involving 38 countries. Between October 2008 and May 2009, ICCS gathered data from more than 140,000 students studying in Grade 8 (or an equivalent grade, where the average age of pupils was at least 13.5). Pupils sat a test on their knowledge of civic processes and institutions, and also completed a questionnaire providing information on their attitudes, values and family background. These data were supplemented by responses to a separate teacher's questionnaire from over 62,000 teachers in the target grade in the selected schools. This questionnaire captured information on the school context and teaching and learning practices. Additionally, school principals completed a questionnaire providing further information on the school's characteristics and context. Regional modules and information from national centres are also available; however, we will only be using data from the pupil and school principal questionnaires in order to address our research questions, as these provide the data necessary for our study.

Data were collected from individuals who were selected in line with a two-stage sampling procedure designed to be representative of the country's wider population. In the first stage, roughly 150 schools per country were selected, with a total of over 5,300 schools taking part. In the second stage, one (or occasionally two) intact classes from the target grade were chosen at random. While Brese et al. (2011) describe this as an 'effective and efficient sampling approach' (p. 8), it means the resulting student sample has a complex, nested structure and sampling weights are strongly recommended. In our analysis, we will account for these features of the data in the ways described in Chapter 4, Section 3.

For our research, ICCS 2009 offers some particular advantages. It was conducted in order to investigate the ways in which young people in countries around the world are prepared to undertake their role as citizens (Ainley, Schulz, & Friedman, 2013). It is therefore directly linked to our topic of study and offers information on many measures relevant to our research questions. The study gathers data on 13- and 14-year-old pupils. This is precisely the age group previously identified as most crucial for the formation of political identity (Janmaat & Hoskins, 2021; see Chapter 2, Section 3). As for the countries involved, of the 38 countries which took part, 24 are in Europe and 21 are in the EU. Conveniently for our purposes, Europe is therefore disproportionately represented. This facilitates comparison between European countries, grouped according to the theoretical framework outlined in the literature section. Moreover, each country has a student sample of 3,000–5,000 students. This large sample size makes it possible to analyse patterns within individual countries, as well as between groups of countries. The quality of the data is extremely high because stringent thresholds were put in place by IEA. For instance, a participation rate of 85% (of schools and pupils within schools) was required in order for the country's results to be included in the final data file. This minimises the risk of a bias in the samples that might come from differential non-participation. Finally, it is a major advantage that data were collected at both the school and individual levels because our analytical unit varies between these depending on which hypothesis we are testing. We are therefore able to derive two separate dependent variables from the data: one at the individual level and one at the school level.

There do exist two more recent cycles of the ICCS survey (2016 and 2022) but the 2009 one was most suited to our research. The ICCS 2022 study had not been released at the time of writing. We decided to use the 2009 study in preference to the 2016 dataset because the latter did not include as many countries of interest for our research as the 2009 survey. Specifically, we were able to include 21 EU countries using the 2009 dataset, whereas only 13 countries would have been eligible for inclusion from the 2016 dataset. It was important for our research to include as many EU countries as possible in order to construct the variable 'political cultures'. In our research, we distinguish between five political systems: Nordic, Liberal, Mediterranean, Conservative and Eastern European (see Table 2). Each political system is represented by two or more countries in our research. The Liberal culture is represented by England and Ireland. Neither of these two countries is included in the 2016 dataset. The Conservative culture is represented by Austria, Luxembourg and the Netherlands. Neither Austria nor Luxembourg is included in the 2016 dataset. The Mediterranean regime is composed of France, Spain, Italy, Greece, Portugal and Malta. While the 2009 dataset includes Spain, Greece, Italy and Malta, the 2016 dataset only includes Italy and Malta. It would therefore have not been possible to include the Liberal political culture using the 2016 dataset, the Conservative culture would have included only the Netherlands and the Mediterranean one would have been represented only by Italy and Malta. Hence, using the 2009 dataset permitted us to carry out a comparative analysis to assess the influence of political systems on school council participation. This would not have been possible using the 2016 data.

2 Variables

This section serves to explain our selection of variables for the purposes of testing our hypotheses and addressing our research questions. The full wording for the questions and response categories from which each variable was derived can be found in the Appendix. The table in the Appendix also specifies whether question data came from the school questionnaires (completed by school principals) or the pupil questionnaire (completed by individual pupils).

2.1 *Dependent Variables*

Our study makes use of two dependent variables which measure access to school councils, allowing us to analyse the determinants of school council access at the level of both individuals and schools.

Dependent Variable 1 (DV1) is at the school level: it is a binary variable measuring whether or not a school has a school council. An item which asked this question directly was not available, therefore we are using a question which asks about the number of students that elect their class representatives. It seems that if at least some students elect class representatives, this means that there is a form of student representation at the school. Conversely, if the principal indicates the question is not applicable or nearly none participate, this suggests that there is no active student representation at the school. We coded some student representation as 1, indicating the existence of a school council, and no student representation as 0 to create a binary variable. As discussed in Chapter 2, Section 1, the nature of the data means we are unable to distinguish between different types of school councils using this measure; some may involve adults, while others may be student-only spaces. While the indicator is therefore not ideal, it provides us with the information we need for our analysis.

Dependent Variable 2 (DV2) is at the individual level: it measures the level of individuals' participation on the school council. It is derived from responses to a question that asks whether or not the respondent has ever been a representative on a school council. When we refer to participation on a council, we therefore refer to being a representative, as opposed to merely voting for representatives. The three possible response categories (given in the Appendix) constitute a scale of participation, where 0 indicates never having participated, 1 indicates past participation, and 2 indicates recent participation. DV2 is treated as a continuous variable, but we re-code it to a binary variable for (only) Chapter 5, Section 4, where we look at the bivariate associations between each individual-level independent variable and individuals' participation graphically; recoding DV2 as a binary variable for this section facilitates the interpretation of the graphs. The re-coding is described in Table 1.

2.2 Independent Variables
2.2.1 National Level
2.2.1.1 Political Culture

In order to measure the impact of national political culture on access to school councils, we have grouped the EU countries for which data is available in ICCS according to their political cultures. This grouping is based on the characterisations of political cultures in Europe discussed in Chapter 3, Section 1. We have excluded Belgium from the analysis, despite its being part of the EU, because only the Flemish region of the country took part in ICCS and thus it was not a representative sample for the country. Based on the literature reviewed in Chapter 3, Section 1, we have constructed the variable 'political culture', which contains five dummy variables: Nordic; Liberal; Mediterranean; Conservative; and eastern European. In Table 2, we present the countries classified in each group. This variable will be used to explore hypotheses 1 and 2.

TABLE 1   Re-code of DV2 into binary dependent variable

Category	N	Valid %	Original coding	New coding
Yes	28393	41.5	2, 3	1
No	40052	58.5	1	0

TABLE 2   Country groupings for the variable 'political culture'

Political culture	Countries
Nordic (N)	Denmark (DNK), Finland (FIN), Sweden (SWE)
Liberal (L)	England (ENG), Ireland (IRL)
Mediterranean (M)	Cyprus (CYP), Spain (ESP), Greece (GRC), Italy (ITA), Malta (MLT)
Conservative (C)	Austria (AUT), Luxembourg (LUX), Netherlands (NLD)
Eastern European (E)	Bulgaria (BGR), Czechia (CZE), Estonia (EST), Lithuania (LTU), Latvia (LVA), Poland (POL), Slovakia (SVK), Slovenia (SVN)

2.2.2 School Level
2.2.2.1 *Elite Schooling*

To test hypothesis 3, we use data from the school questionnaire answering whether the school is private or public. We have coded public schools as 0 and private schools as 1. It should be noted that a private school is defined on the questionnaire as any school that is not managed by a public education authority (the exact wording can be found in the Appendix). This means that fee-paying schools are considered only a subcategory of private schools in ICCS. There may, for example, be private schools managed by the church which are not fee-paying. However, we suggest that it should sufficiently capture the concept of elite schooling. A common feature of private schools in the countries involved is increased autonomy in relation to teaching, learning and values (Ainley, Schulz, & Friedman, 2013). This increases the likelihood of such schools having a distinct school ethos which may have the potential to develop different citizens.

2.2.2.2 *School's Social Composition*

To test hypotheses 4 and 7, a composite measure of individuals' social background (described below) was used to measure the social composition of a school. We calculated the mean score for social background for each class:[1] a lower score indicates that many students are of low SES, while a higher score indicates that the school has more pupils from an advantaged background.

2.2.2.3 *School's Ethnic Composition*

In order to explore the impact of ethnicity at the school level (hypotheses 5 and 11), we have adapted the measure of individual ethnicity (described below). As with social composition, we take the mean of the ethnicity scores in each class: a mean close to 1 indicates more ethnic minority students, while a mean score closer to 0 indicates a higher proportion of ethnic majority students. An important limitation to note is that the question on ethnicity was an optional item on the questionnaire; only 9 of the EU countries chose to include it.[2] This means that we are missing data on this item for some countries; they have been excluded from our analysis when investigating the influence of ethnicity on access to school councils.

2.2.3 Individual Level
2.2.3.1 *Social Background*

To explore the impact of social background on access (hypotheses 6, 7 and 10), we are using a composite indicator designed to measure SES. This indicator is composed of three items: the education level of the respondent's father, the same for the mother, and the number of books in the respondent's home. The education level is measured on a scale from 1-6, where 1 signals a degree or equivalent and 6 signals the non-completion of ISCED level 1 (primary education). The number of books in the home is also measured on a scale from 1-6, where 1 signals 0-10 books and 6 signals more than 500 books. We have coded these three indicators so that a higher number always indicates higher SES (i.e. reversed the coding for education level). We then take the mean of the three variables to give a final SES score for each individual, where a higher score indicates higher SES. Of course, this variable measures a respondent's *parents'* education level and number of books and thus is conceptually distinct from the respondent's personal aspirations and choices. While these are often connected (Burns, Verba, & Schlozman, 2003), it is also important to include a measure of personal aspirations, as we do below.

2.2.3.2 *Personal Aspirations*
The educational aspirations of pupils will be captured by what level of education the pupil respondent expects to complete. The item used offers options ranging from degree level to the non-achievement of 5 GCSEs at pass grade (see Appendix). This will be treated as a continuous variable as the responses have a natural order, with degree level the maximum possible score and fewer than 5 GCSEs as the lowest possible score. This variable will be used to test hypothesis 8.

2.2.3.3 *Ethnicity*
The ethnic background of an individual will be measured by responses to a question asking pupils their ethnicity on the student questionnaire. We derived a binary variable from these responses, with pupils either part of the national ethnic majority or an ethnic minority group in their country. We have coded the national ethnic majority as 0, with all other options (ethnic minority groups) coded as 1. This variable will be used to test hypotheses 9, 10 and 11.

2.2.3.4 *Gender*
We will test the link between gender and access to school councils (hypothesis 12) using the binary indicator of female/male. The data for this variable comes from the student questionnaire, and thus measures pupils' gender self-identification.

Table 3 offers the descriptive statistics of all the variables included in the analysis.

TABLE 3   Descriptive data for all dependent and independent variables

Level	Variable	Variable type	Valid N	N in category	Valid %	Mean	SD	Min	Max
School	DV1 – Does the school have a council?	Binary	3470						
	Yes			2817	81.2				
	No			653	18.8				
Individual	DV2 – Have you been a representative on the council?	Continuous	68445			1.63	0.81	1	3
Country	Political culture	Categorical	21						
	Nordic			3	14.3				
	Liberal			2	9.5				
	Mediterranean			5	23.8				
	Conservative			3	14.3				
	Eastern			8	38.1				
School	Elite schooling	Binary	3104						
	Public			2760	88.9				
	Private			344	11.1				
School	SES composition	Continuous	3469			0.48	0.48	−1.41	2.08
School	Ethnic composition	Continuous	1441			0.21	0.26	0.00	1.00
Individual	SES	Continuous	66706			0.52	0.87	−2.15	2.2
Individual	Ethnicity	Binary	27599						
	Majority			22015	79.8				
	Minority			5584	20.2				
Individual	Expected education	Continuous	67880			3.03	1.028	0	4
Individual	Gender	Binary	68690						
	Female			34500	50.2				
	Male			34190	49.8				

3   Method

We will use SPSS, version 25.0 (IBM Corp., 2017) to analyse the quantitative data from ICCS 2009. Our aim is to discover the determinants of access to school councils at three levels (national, school and individual) so that we can first ascertain whether access is unequal (Chapter 5) and, second, discuss the implications if it is (Chapter 6). We will therefore begin by presenting statistics, using DV1, on the frequency of school councils in the different political cultures (Chapter 5, Section 2). DV1 is appropriate for this analysis because this research question is concerned with how many schools offer the opportunity to participate on a school council, rather than how many pupils have taken part within these schools. This initial analysis will show whether students living in different political cultures have differential access to school councils.

In order to investigate the school characteristics associated with different levels of access, we will again use DV1. We will carry out a logistic regression analysis in order to find which school characteristics increase the likelihood of the school having a council (Chapter 5, Section 3). This method is appropriate as DV1 is a binary outcome (either the school has a council, or it does not).

For the individual-level analysis, we will begin by exploring the bivariate associations between each individual-level independent variable and DV2 (Chapter 5, Section 4). As mentioned, DV2 is re-coded to create a binary variable for this analysis. The aim is to gain an initial idea of whether the relationships anticipated in the literature review are reflected in the data, and to reveal any unusual patterns in the bivariate associations that might influence the main analysis, described below.

We will then move onto the main analysis to discover the determinants of access to school councils at the individual level, using DV2 (Chapter 5, Section 5). Since the data have a nested structure, and DV2 is a continuous variable, we will conduct a linear multilevel analysis (MLA), which is an appropriate method for handling hierarchical data structures (Bock, 1989). The data is at three levels: individual (Level 1); class/school (Level 2); and country (Level 3). we will use the recommended sampling weights for students throughout our analysis. It is also possible to include interaction effects in a MLA, which is necessary to test hypotheses 10 and 11. In the models including interaction effects, we use standardised forms of the variables included in the interaction: the continuous variables are centred so that the mean is 0 for each.

Notes

1   We recognise that there is some conflation between school and class in our analysis and this was necessary because the data are in fact nested at four levels: country, school, class

and individual. Since having four levels poses some serious difficulties for the analysis of the data, we have eliminated the school level by treating each class as a separate school. There is generally only one class from each school included in the data set and this therefore mostly makes no difference to the data. In the rare cases that there are two classes from a school, they will in effect be treated as two different schools. This same principle is applied to the measurement of ethnic composition of schools.

2   The countries that do provide data on ethnicity are Slovenia, Netherlands, Latvia, Luxembourg, Greece, Finland, Estonia, England and Cyprus.

CHAPTER 5

Results

Determinants of Access to School Councils across Europe

1   The Empty Model

Our first analysis was a three-level linear regression model for DV2 including no predictor variables. This so-called empty model for clustered data calculates the *proportion* of the variance at the country, school and individual levels (Heck, Thomas, & Tabata, 2014).

The results show that 80.7% of the variance is at the individual level; 9.6% of the variance is at the school level; and 9.7% of the variance is at the country level ($p < 0.005$ for all, suggesting high statistical significance). These results justify a closer analysis at each level to better understand the determinants of variance (Lee, 2000; Garson, 2013). The results also justify using a three-level MLA as the nested structure of the data has a clear effect on the distribution of variance.

2   Country Level Analysis

In this section, we investigate access to school councils where access is conceptualised as availability. That is, we explore what proportion of schools within each country – and within each political culture – have a school council. Overall in the EU, 81.2% (SE = 0.007) of schools do have a school council, while 18.8% (SE = 0.007) do not. Further analysis reveals that the proportion of schools with a council varies significantly between countries. Figure 1 shows the proportion of schools within each country – and within each political culture – with a council. As can be seen, Italy has the lowest percentage of schools with a council (only 29.3%), which is 51.9 percentage points below the European average of 81.2%. Poland appears to have the highest proportion, with 100% of schools reporting student representation. This is surprising given the expectation of low democratic participation in eastern European countries that emerged from the literature review, and will be discussed below. While Italy and Poland are the two extremes, the majority of schools appear to be roughly in line with the EU average: only four countries (ITA, BGR, NLD and LUX) have a percentage below 76.3% (i.e. more than five percentage points

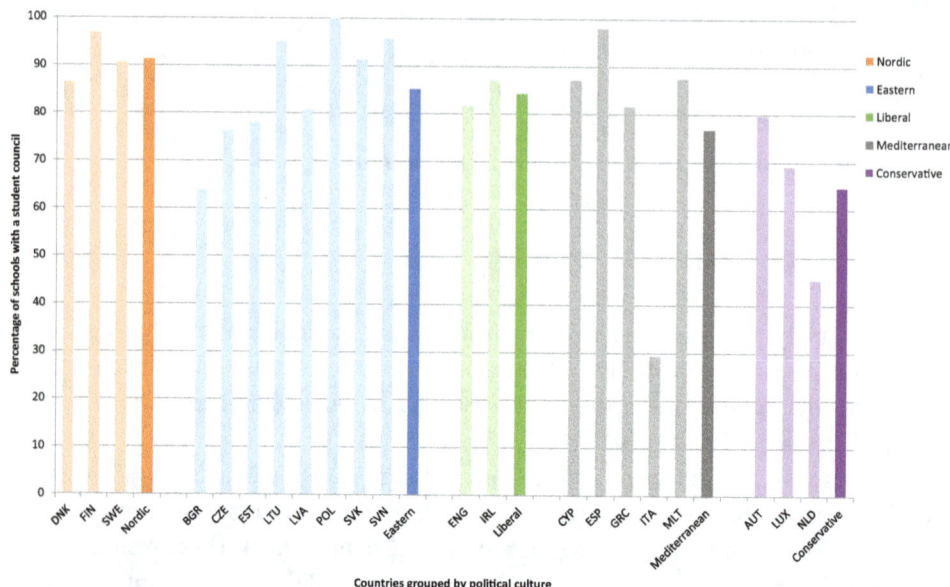

FIGURE 1   Percentage of schools with a council within each country and political culture

below the average). This indicates a pattern of general convergence with some outliers.

The darker bar in each group in Figure 1 shows the average percentage of schools with a council within that culture. It can be seen that the Nordic countries have the highest average percentage at 91.2%. This means that, across this political culture, 91.2% of schools have a school council. Conversely, the Conservative countries have the lowest levels of access to school councils, with 64.6% of schools offering a council. The political culture with the second highest percentage is the eastern European culture. Hypothesis 1 appears to be somewhat undermined by these results. While the prediction regarding the Nordic and Conservative countries appears justified, eastern European countries appear to have many opportunities for participating on school councils (specifically, at 85.1% of schools).

The Liberal countries appear to be in the middle in terms of the proportion of schools with a council, with an average of 84.3%. This figure is only slightly below the eastern European countries, which suggests that it is important to test whether the difference is statistically significant and likely to say something meaningful about the difference between the two cultures, or rather the result of sampling. We have therefore carried out tests to determine the statistical significance of the results, discussed below.

The Mediterranean political culture has the fourth highest proportion of schools with councils, with an average of 76.7%. This group does not, however, appear very cohesive. Italy appears to be an outlier in this group, which has lowered the average. Without Italy, the Mediterranean group would have an average of 88.6%, which would have made it the political culture with the second highest proportion of school councils (after the Nordic countries). The Conservative political culture also appears somewhat incohesive, with a range of 34.4 percentage points (AUT = 79.6%; NLD = 45.2%). A lack of cohesiveness is important to note in this analysis, as it may signal that the theoretical country groupings are not justified by the empirical data. In the next section, we will therefore consider reasons for the lack of cohesiveness in these two cultures.

The Welch test (Lewis-Beck, Bryman, & Liao, 2004) confirms that the difference between group means is statistically significant ($F(4, 1178.66) = 31.08$, $p < 0.000$). The Games-Howell post-hoc test determines precisely which groups do and do not have a statistically significant difference of means. It can be seen that the following cultures do *not*: Liberal and Nordic; Liberal and eastern; Conservative and Mediterranean ($p > 0.05$). For all other groups, there appears to be a significant difference between the means ($p < 0.05$), suggesting there is genuinely differential access to school councils between these cultures. This can also be seen in Figure 2, which shows the means and 95% confidence interval bands for the five political cultures. Where the confidence intervals overlap, the means are not significantly different.

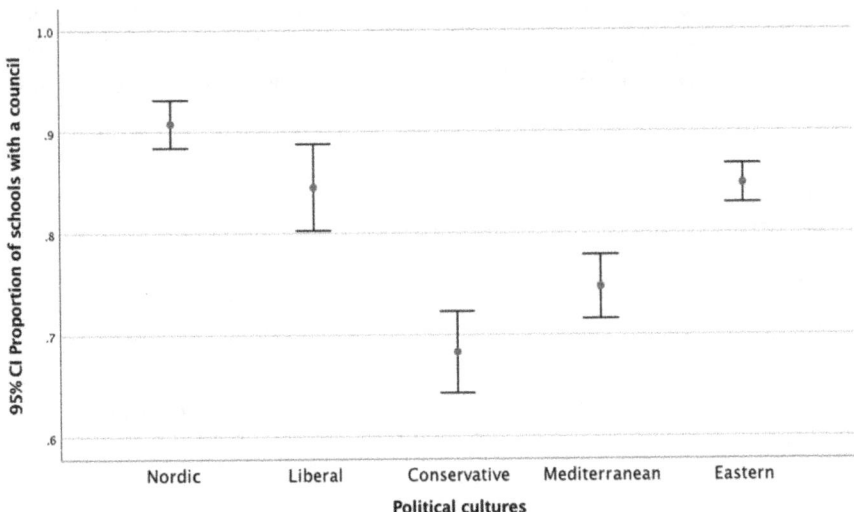

FIGURE 2   Proportion of schools (with 95% confidence intervals) with a council within five political cultures

3   School Level Analysis

Before conducting the multilevel analysis which takes account of the nested structure of the data, we explored the relationships between school level predictors (private/public; SES composition; ethnic composition) and the school level dependent variable, DV1. Our aim was to see what kinds of schools are more likely to have a school council across the EU. We carried out a logistic regression analysis because DV1 is a binary outcome (either the school has a council, or it does not). The results of this analysis are shown in Table 4. Model 1 includes all the countries in the dataset. Model 2 includes only those nine countries for which there are data on ethnicity (specified in Chapter 4) and uses the same syntax as Model 1. It was important to run Model 2 because the valid N (the number of schools included in the analysis) decreases substantially when only nine countries are used. In order to properly understand the influence of ethnic composition, Model 2 was needed for comparison to show which changes were the result of including this variable, and which were due

TABLE 4   Determinants of school council availability at the school level

Variable	Model 1			Model 2			Model 3		
	B	S.E.	B(Exp)	B	S.E.	B(Exp)	B	S.E.	B(Exp)
Constant	1.810**	0.073	6.113	3.077**	0.213	21.703	2.958**	0.270	19.266
Private[a]	−0.330	0.19	0.714	−1.252**	0.358	0.286	−1.269**	0.360	0.281
SES composition	1.021**	0.128	2.776	0.279	0.298	1.321	0.353	0.321	1.423
Ethnic composition							0.417	0.605	1.517
Nagelkerke R Square	0.043			0.029			0.031		
Hosmer and Lemeshow test	$p = 0.021$			$p = 0.040$			$p = 0.916$		
Model coefficients	$\chi^2 = 64.491$, df = 2, $p < 0.000$			$\chi^2 = 10.888$, df = 2, $p < 0.005$			$\chi^2 = 11.384$, df = 3, $p = 0.01$		
Valid N	3104			1209			1209		

**$p < 0.005$

a   The reference category is 'public'.

RESULTS

to the change in the dataset. Model 3 then includes just the countries with ethnicity data and the additional independent variable of the school's ethnic composition.

Model 1 appears to show a statistically significant and positive association between a school's SES composition and the likelihood of having a council (B = 1.021, $p < 0.005$). The odds ratio suggests that an increase of one unit in the SES composition score increases the odds of the school having a school council by 2.776. This means that a school which is one SES composition unit above the average is almost three times more likely than a school with average SES composition to have a school council. This finding appears to support hypothesis 4 (*Schools with a high proportion of low SES pupils are less likely to have a school council than schools with a high SES composition*). However, it will be interesting to observe whether the SES composition of a school remains an important explanatory variable when analysing school access at the individual level and taking account of the nested structure of the data (Chapter 5, Section 5).

Model 1 also shows the perhaps surprising result that private schools are less likely than public schools to have a council (B = −0.337). This would appear to oppose hypothesis 3. However, this result is not statistically significant ($p > 0.05$) and so it may be that public schools are no more likely than private schools to have a council. The logistic regression analysis for Model 1 generated a predicted probability, for each school, of having a school council. Figure 3

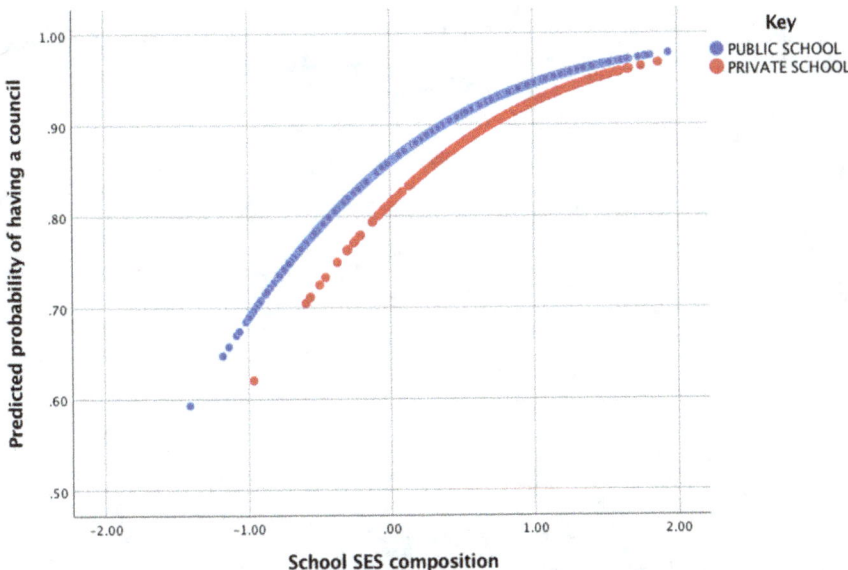

FIGURE 3   Predicted probability of having a school council by school type (1)

provides a visual representation of this analysis, showing the change in predicted probability associated with a change in a school's SES composition. The scatterplot shows a clear positive association between the predicted probability of having a council and SES composition. The predicted probability increases in a curvilinear fashion until the higher end of SES score, where the slope begins to flatten: schools with any SES composition score of over 1 appear to have a similar predicted probability to each other. This is due to the binary nature of the outcome; as the probability nears 1, SES composition makes less difference. We have included the private school variable for interest, even though it should be viewed with caution due to low statistical significance. The scatterplot shows that a private school must have a higher SES composition score than a public school in order to achieve the same predicted probability.

The results of Model 2 (shown in Table 4) show that, for the subset of nine countries, the effect of a school's SES composition is not statistically significant ($p > 0.05$), while the effect of being a private or public school is statistically significant ($p < 0.005$). Private schools appear to be less likely than public schools to have a council ($B = -1.269$). This indicates a different story to the EU-wide data (Model 1). It appears that the determinants of school council access at the school level are different in these nine countries. This highlights the need to consider country-specific explanations for patterns of access, where possible. We do this in Chapter 6.

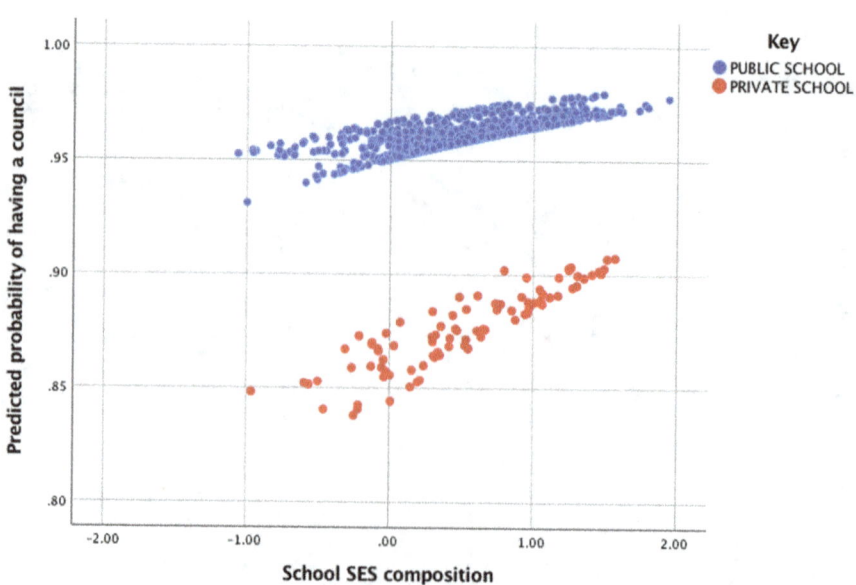

FIGURE 4   Predicted probability of having a school council by school type (2)

When the school level ethnicity indicator is included, the private school indicator remains statistically significant and the SES indicator remains insignificant. The influence of the school's ethnic composition appears not to be a statistically significant predictor of school council access. This therefore suggests that hypothesis 5 (*Schools with a high proportion of ethnic minority pupils are less likely to have a school council*) is unsupported by this analysis. The predicted probabilities generated by Model 3 are shown in Figure 4 and it can be seen that including the effect of ethnic composition in the model leads to a wider spread of predicted probabilities.

4   Initial Observations at the Individual Level

We explored the bivariate associations across the whole of the EU between each of the individual-level predictor variables and the individual-level dependent variable, DV2 (see Table 1 for our re-coding of DV2 for this section). We did this to draw out any unusual patterns in the data that might further illuminate how socio-demographic factors influence levels of school council participation. Figure 5 presents the graphs from this analysis. The y-axis on all graphs shows the percentage of students that have participated on a school council at some point. Because a more in-depth analysis – taking account of the nested data structure – is presented in Chapter 5, Section 5, we will mention only briefly that girls initially appear to participate slightly more than boys, while pupils from ethnic majority and minority backgrounds appear to participate at very similar levels.

The line graphs in Figure 5, however, show patterns of particular interest. The line graph showing the association between expected education and participation indicates that the proportion of pupils who have been on a council is highest for those who expect to achieve the highest level of education (almost 49%). However, there is a somewhat puzzling dip in the graph representing a low participation rate amongst those that expect to achieve a middling amount of education (32.5%). This suggests the relationship is more complex than a straightforward positive, linear association between expected education and participation on councils. The MLA is not able to reveal this so clearly because it generates information about the overall pattern. Looking at the bivariate association has therefore highlighted a relationship that may otherwise have remained hidden.

The line graph showing the bivariate association between participation and SES appears to reveal a generally positive correlation, although there is a considerable amount of variation within this (shown by frequent and large spikes). The line tends towards higher participation rates for higher SES students.

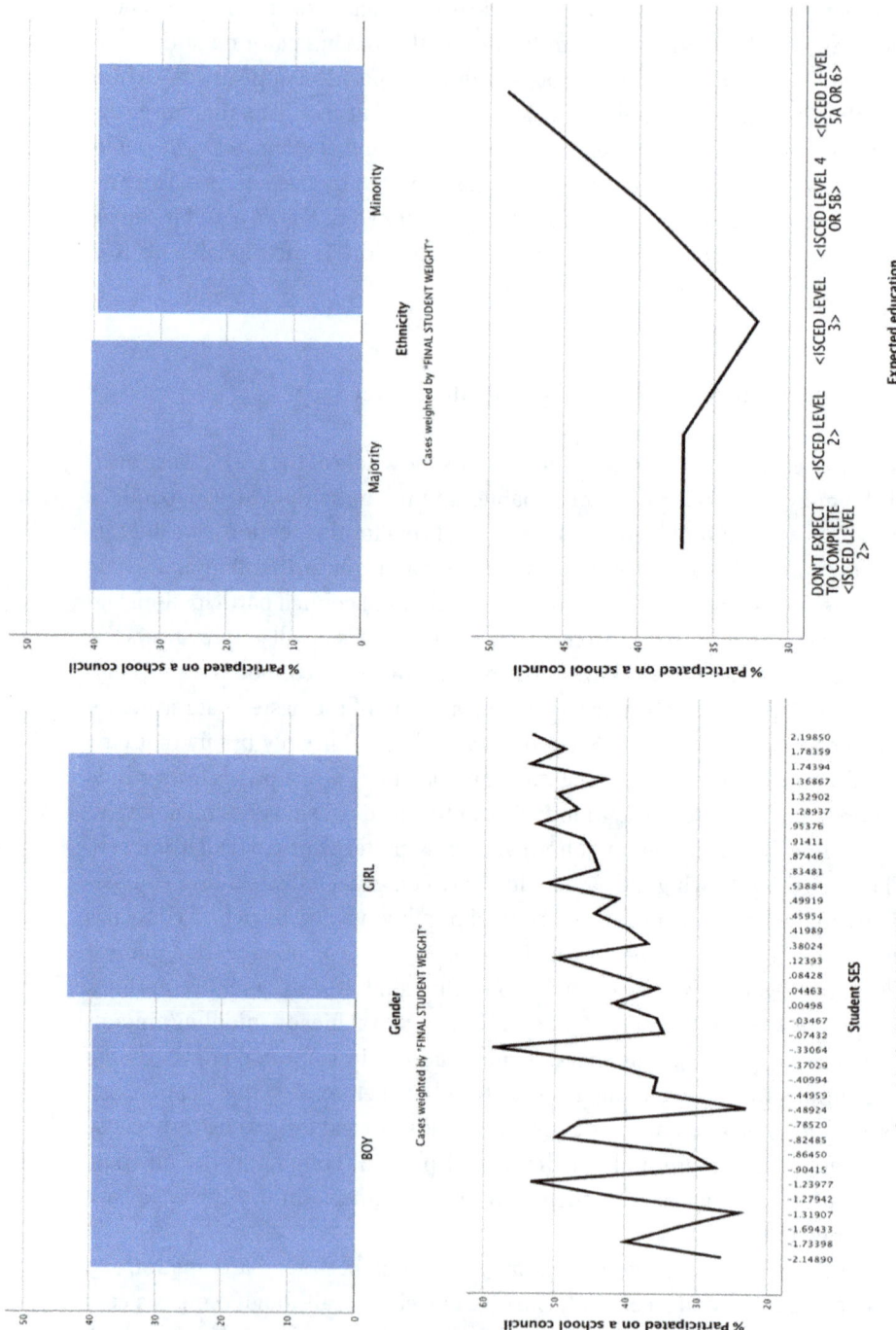

FIGURE 5 Bivariate associations between pupil characteristics and participation on the school council

Furthermore, this trend appears to be more consistent as SES score increases, shown by the smaller spikes towards the higher end of the x-axis. The large spikes at the lower end of the x-axis suggest participation rates of low SES students are variable.

5   Determinants of Individuals' Participation (Multi-Level Analysis)

In order to determine the factors that influence individuals' access to school councils, we conducted a three-level linear multilevel regression analysis using DV2 to take account of the hierarchical data structure (Heck, Thomas, & Tabata, 2014). The results are presented in Table 5. Model 1 uses the full dataset and therefore does not include the variables tapping ethnicity (12 countries did not provide these data). Models 2, 3 and 4 include only the nine countries for which there are data on ethnicity. Model 2 uses the same variables as Model 1 so that the effect of adding the ethnicity indicators for those nine countries in Model 3 can be seen clearly; Model 3 includes the variables tapping ethnicity; and Model 4 includes interaction effects to test hypotheses 10 and 11.

As country level predictors, we included the five political cultures as dummy variables in all models. It can be seen that none of these reached near statistical significance. In order to investigate further the influence of political culture on individuals' access to councils (to test hypothesis 2), we have carried out a further MLA including just one country from each political culture. This analysis is justified further at the end of this chapter and the results are presented in Table 6.

The explained variance (R^2) for each level of the model is stated at the bottom of Table 5. It can be seen that the models explain only a modest proportion of the variance at the individual level, for instance Model 1 explains just 2.7% of the variance at Level 1. Possible reasons for this will be discussed in Section 7.

Despite the small R^2 values at the individual level, the results of the MLA reveal some clear and statistically significant patterns. Model 1 indicates that all the independent variables except the political cultures and private school indicators have a highly statistically significant effect on individuals' participation ($p < 0.005$). The insignificance of the private school variable confirms the finding of the logistic regression analysis (Chapter 5, Section 3): there does not appear to be an association between elite schooling and increased access to councils.

We turn now to the effect of SES on school council participation. It can be seen in Model 1 that individuals with higher SES are associated with increased participation. Specifically, pupils of high SES are associated with a one-sixth

TABLE 5   Determinants of individuals' participation on the school council in EU countries

Level	Variable	Model 1 B	Model 1 SE	Model 1 t	Model 2 B	Model 2 SE	Model 2 t	Model 3 B	Model 3 SE	Model 3 t	Model 4 B	Model 4 SE	Model 4 t
	Intercept	1.333**	(0.054)	25.7	1.237**	(0.211)	5.9	1.291**	(0.215)	6	1.213**	(0.210)	5.8
1	Gender[a]	0.033**	(0.001)	34.3	0.063**	(0.002)	33.0	0.062**	(0.002)	32.4	0.061**	(0.002)	32.1
1	Expected edu.	0.072**	(0.001)	143.6	0.093**	(0.001)	89.1	0.093**	(0.001)	89.4	0.094**	(0.001)	89.5
1	SES	0.078**	(0.001)	124.1	0.108**	(0.001)	91.3	0.109**	(0.001)	91.4	0.110**	(0.001)	84.2
2	Private[b]	−0.031	(0.020)	−1.6	−0.016	(0.045)	−0.4	−0.009	(0.046)	−0.2	−0.013	(0.046)	−0.3
2	School SES	−0.055**	(0.008)	−6.6	−0.117**	(0.014)	−8.4	−0.160**	(0.015)	−10.9	−0.157**	(0.015)	−10.7
3	Eastern[c]	0.057	(0.176)	0.3	0.131	(0.244)	0.5	0.170	(0.248)	0.7	0.170	(0.243)	0.7
3	Liberal[c]	−0.085	(0.238)	−0.4	0.002	(0.299)	0.0	0.047	(0.304)	0.2	0.042	(0.298)	0.1
3	Mediterranean[c]	0.191	(0.190)	1.0	0.584	(0.259)	2.3	0.609	(0.263)	2.3	0.599	(0.258)	2.3
3	Conservative[c]	0.037	(0.214)	0.2	−0.100	(0.261)	−0.4	−0.037	(0.265)	−0.1	−0.043	(0.260)	−0.2
1	Ethnicity[d]							−0.013**	(0.003)	−4.7	0.010**	(0.003)	3.1
2	School ethnicity							−0.347**	(0.030)	−11.6	−0.274**	(0.030)	−9.0
1	SES* ethnicity										−0.006*	(0.003)	−2.5
Mixed	Ethnicity* school ethnicity										−0.179**	(0.013)	−14.1
R²: L1; L2; L3		0.027; −0.048; −0.070			0.040; −0.027; 0.547			0.040; −0.095; 0.532			0.040; −0.104; 0.550		

*p < 0.05; **p < 0.005
a The reference category is 'boy'.
b The reference category is 'public'.
c The reference category is 'Nordic'.
d The reference category is 'ethnic majority'.

RESULTS

TABLE 6 Determinants of individuals' participation on the school council in five countries

Level	Variable	Latvia B	SE	t	The Netherlands B	SE	t	Finland B	SE	t	England B	SE	t	Greece B	SE	t
	Intercept	1.435**	0.043	33.1	1.141**	0.072	15.8	1.192**	0.397	3.0	1.312**	0.093	14.0	1.739**	0.052	33.2
1	Gender[a]	0.122**	0.011	11.1	−0.007	0.004	−1.9	0.107**	0.006	17.6	0.107**	0.003	41.0	−0.101**	0.006	−17.1
1	Expected edu.	0.063**	0.006	10.4	0.092**	0.003	33.2	0.078**	0.003	24.2	0.090**	0.001	66.7	0.128**	0.004	35.9
1	Ethnicity[b]	−0.023	0.021	−1.1	0.069**	0.006	11.2	0.148**	0.015	10.1	−0.030**	0.004	−8.4	−0.079**	0.010	−8.2
1	SES	0.070**	0.008	9.0	0.048**	0.003	17.7	0.076**	0.004	17.7	0.149**	0.002	97.0	0.028**	0.004	7.3
2	Private[c]	0.029	0.222	0.1	−0.101	0.083	−1.2	−0.099	0.131	−0.8	−0.185	0.217	−0.9	−0.111	0.110	−1.0
2	School SES	−0.133**	0.045	−3.0	−0.048**	0.003	−7.1	−0.013	0.062	−0.2	0.272*	0.114	2.4	0.040	0.065	0.6
2	School ethnicity	0.205**	0.082	2.5	−0.025	0.124	−0.2	−0.125	0.095	1.3	−1.455**	0.113	−12.9	0.247	0.261	1.0
Valid N (unweighted)		2761			1964			3307			2916			3153		

*p < 0.05; **p < 0.005
a The reference category is 'boy'.
b The reference category is 'ethnic majority'.
c The reference category is 'public'.

higher amount of participation than those of low SES. This finding is highly statistically significant (t = 124.1, p < 0.005). This provides good support for hypothesis 6.

This finding is, however, complicated somewhat by the negative association between school SES composition and participation (B = −0.055) shown in Model 1. This means that higher SES composition scores (schools where pupils are on average of higher SES) are associated with individuals participating less. This is an interesting finding and may appear to conflict with the findings of the logistic regression, which found schools with high SES composition more likely to have a school council. However, it should be noted that the logistic regression analysis used DV1, which is a school level variable. This MLA uses DV2 and therefore explores access patterns for individuals. Therefore, considered together, the results of both analyses suggest that schools with high SES composition are more likely to offer a council, but an individual student of a given SES participates less at schools with high SES composition. Campbell (2006) suggests that this may be evidence of education having a positional effect on participation as it implies that individuals' participation level is reduced by being amongst others of high SES. This may provide support for hypothesis 7. However, since the effect of individual SES is stronger than the effect of school SES (shown by the respective t-values), the positional theory is only slightly supported (ibid.): it seems that an individual's SES has more of an absolute effect, which is important even when school SES composition is included in the model.

At the individual level in Model 1, it can be seen that girls are associated with higher rates of participation than boys (B = 0.033, t = 34.3, p < 0.005). This effect size is small but statistically significant and therefore aligns with the findings of the bivariate associations (Figure 5). Hypothesis 12 is therefore not overwhelmingly supported by this analysis; however, it seems that the participation gap between boys and girls is only very small.

With regards to the effect of expected education level, Model 1 shows that the effect size of expected education level is fairly similar to the effect of SES. This is also reflected in the similar t-value (for expected education, t = 143.6, p < 0.005). The positive association, relatively large effect size and statistical significance of this independent variable provides strong support for hypothesis 8. However, it should again be noted that the bivariate association analysis revealed a non-linear relationship between expected education and DV2, which will be discussed in Section 7. Overall, the t-values for SES and expected education are the highest two out of the explanatory variables in Model 1, suggesting that these two indicators are the most important predictors in the model.

RESULTS

Model 2 shows the results of the MLA using only the nine countries which provide data on ethnicity. The R^2 values suggest that ethnicity is an important indicator to include when investigating access patterns to school councils. Ethnic minority has been coded as 1, therefore Model 3 shows a small negative average effect of being an ethnic minority on participation (B = −0.013, t = −4.7, p < 0.005). That is, those from an ethnic minority background have just slightly lower levels of access to school councils. In contrast, the effect of the school level ethnicity variable is striking. Schools with high ethnic minority composition are associated with a large and statistically significant decline in individuals' participation on councils (B = −0.347, t = −1.6, p < 0.005). In other words, individuals in a school with only ethnic majority pupils are associated with over one-sixth higher DV2 value than individuals in schools with only ethnic minority pupils.

The significance of the interaction effect between ethnicity and school ethnic composition included in Model 4 suggests that the effect of being from an ethnic minority background depends on the school type the individual attends (B = −0.179, t = −14.1, p < 0.005). Ethnic minority pupils at schools with more ethnic minority students have lower rates of participation than their counterparts at ethnic majority schools. In addition, the difference in participation levels between ethnic majority and ethnic minority students is larger in schools with more minority students. That is, the negative effect of being an ethnic minority pupil is compounded by attending a school with other ethnic minority students, providing support for hypothesis 11. The interaction effect between ethnicity and SES is statistically significant (p < 0.05) and negative. This suggests that the difference in participation levels between ethnic majority and ethnic minority students is smaller among the high SES students. This provides support for hypothesis 10.

Finally, Table 6 shows the results of a MLA using data from five individual countries. It can be seen that there is one country from each political culture. The aim was to investigate further the influence of political culture on patterns of access to school councils amongst individuals and therefore to test hypothesis 2. Unfortunately, it was not possible to run the MLA on all the countries in the political culture because of the lack of data for the majority of countries. Having observed the importance of the ethnicity variables (their high statistical significance and the increased R^2 of models that include them), we judged that it would be most informative to include ethnicity variables, at the expense of having to choose just one country from each culture. We used Figure 1 to help our selection of countries: we tried to choose a country that was representative (i.e. close to the average) of each culture. We also chose a country with a large enough sample size to make the findings reliable. (This excluded

Luxembourg, for example. Brese et al. (2011, p. 32) state that MLA is not recommended for this country due to the small number of participating schools.) As a result of carrying out the MLA on one country at a time, it was also meaningless to include the political cultures as dummy variables and so these have been excluded.

It can be seen that the individual level predictors all have a statistically significant effect on participation, with the sole exception of gender in the Netherlands. This opposes hypothesis 2, which suggested that differences in participation levels based on individuals' socio-economic characteristics would be smaller in the Nordic countries. Yet even if there remain statistically significant differences, the direction of the associations should be noted: there is a particularly strong *positive* association between school council participation and being an ethnic minority in Finland, but a statistically significant and *negative* association in England and Greece. This suggests that minority groups may be more included and represented in the Nordic countries, providing some support for hypothesis 2. SES and expected education have the expected positive relationship in all five countries.

Moving now to school-level predictors, it is striking that none of these is statistically significant in Finland or Greece. This suggests that access to school councils in these countries is not influenced by the school types included in our analysis. This is in sharp contrast to England, where the effect of a school's SES and ethnic composition is extremely strong. In England, a one unit increase in SES composition is associated with a large rise (B = 0.272) in participation. A higher score for ethnic composition (i.e. more ethnic minority students) is associated with a sharp decline in participation in England (B = –1.480). This would suggest that, in England, pupils at more socially advantaged schools, and at schools with few ethnic minority students, have much greater access to school councils. This corresponds to Campbell's (2006) theory of a cumulative effect of education, whereby individuals' participation levels rise in accordance with their peers' average SES level. The private school indicator is not statistically significant in any of these five countries, which aligns with the previous analyses. In Latvia and the Netherlands, school SES composition is negatively associated with individuals' participation, while individual SES is positively associated with participation, possibly suggesting a slight positional effect in these countries, as in the EU-wide analysis shown in Table 5 (Campbell, 2006; Nie, Junn, & Stehlik-Barry, 1996).

CHAPTER 6

Exclusive Clubs

European Youth Goal 9 aims to promote space and participation in the political sphere for all young people and, in so doing, strengthen the democracies of countries across the EU (European Union, 2018). We argued that school councils may address European Youth Goal 9 for normative and/or pedagogical reasons, addressing the citizenship rights of pupils in the present and/or future. Our three research questions interrogated access at three levels: country, school and individual. On the basis of the literature review, we conceptualised access in two distinct ways. First, we found that a barrier may be simply a lack of availability in the country or school. Second, it may be an inability or unwillingness to participate on the basis of previous developmental experiences. We used the ICCS 2009 as our data source to explore patterns in school council access.

The key finding from the preceding analyses is that there *is* differential access to school councils across Europe, and some variation can be found at all three levels. Moreover, the patterns of access appear to be associated with certain socio-demographic factors, as described in the results chapter. This suggests that differences in access are not random, but rather represent real structural barriers which disadvantage some groups and privilege others. In this chapter, we will discuss the findings, consider explanations for surprising or interesting findings, and draw out some of the possible implications of our results.

1   International Overview

While some countries' access levels diverge significantly from the EU average, it was interesting to note that many countries across Europe have a similar level of access to councils. This suggests that there is some convergence of educational policies on citizenship, despite the different political cultures and different types and ages of democracy that have been identified in Europe (e.g. Kitanova, 2019; Wilensky, 2002). This convergence towards youth political participation strategies has been noted by the European Commission's (2017) Eurydice report: *Citizenship Education at School in Europe*. This report finds that recommendations for school councils are 'almost universal' (p. 38) across all EU countries. The data presented here provide some empirical evidence that the recommendations are also almost universally enacted.

Yet some convergence does not necessarily mean the theoretical distinctions between different kinds of democracy are irrelevant. Helgøy and Homme (2006) note that policy tools in education – such as the means of increasing political participation – can converge while reflecting distinct institutional and cultural contexts. That is, school councils could be the common policy tool chosen for addressing declining youth participation, but with different motivations, reflecting different values and approaches. This finding is supported by Kränzl-Nagl and Zartler (2010), who find that countries across Europe are increasingly promoting youth participation opportunities, but for different reasons. In young democracies, they find an emphasis on influencing political socialisation by offering opportunities to learn the procedures of democracy early. This clearly corresponds to the pedagogical justification explained in Chapter 2, Section 3. On the other hand, more established democracies, such as Norway, have a long-standing tradition of promoting children's participation on the basis of children's rights principles (ibid.). This is an example of the normative justification explained in Chapter 2, Section 2. Thus it is plausible that considering *access* to political participation opportunities will not uncover the deeper differences in citizenship in European countries, which might better be captured by exploring the motivations behind different opportunities. Thus, while our findings may show some convergence, this is perhaps only an aspect of the full story with regards to how and why youth participation is promoted across the EU.

In terms of the outliers, it may be that some countries have a genuinely different approach to promoting democracy (they use different educational tools) or even a genuinely different expectation of how citizens should engage with decision-making. On the other hand, the case of Italy suggests a much simpler explanation may suffice. Our analysis highlighted a strikingly low proportion of schools in Italy with a school council. Walther (2012) explains that school councils in Italy tend to be at the level of the province and are therefore not tied to one particular school. There is evidence that these councils provide useful, practical experience of citizenship outside of school and that their organisation is based on excellent links between the local authorities and schools (Catarci, 2018). Therefore, a better understanding of the structure of youth democracy in Italy shows a pattern of youth engagement that is not captured by our data which focuses on schools as the organising unit. This highlights the need to understand the specific context of a country before drawing conclusions about educational practices on the basis of quantitative data. Unfortunately, it is beyond the scope of this book to delve into the context of each country in depth, but future research could. The case of Italy also emphasises that democratic initiatives for youth need not be the sole responsibility of the school. Further research might explore in more detail the potential for youth engagement outside of school, or in collaboration with schools.

2 The Influence of Political Cultures

We turn now to the variable 'political culture' which we created on the basis of the literature on different kinds of citizenship and democracy within the EU (Chapter 3, Section 1). The observed general convergence combined with some outliers may appear to undermine the idea that distinct political cultures are reflected in school council access. However, it cannot be ignored that the results of the Welch test suggest that there are statistically significant differences between some groups. Most obviously, the data appear to support the existence of a discrete Nordic group of countries with consistently high levels of access to school councils. The literature converged on its expectations for this group, with Wilensky (2002) describing it as neo-corporatist and Walther (2012) observing that students tend to have a status as co-citizens. We therefore hypothesised that pupils in these countries would have increased access to school councils, which indeed they appear to have.

However, there was some conflict in the literature discussed with regards to the political cultures in the remainder of western Europe. While Wilensky's (2002) characterisation of England and Ireland as least-corporatist led to the expectation that these countries would have few structured opportunities for student representation, Green, Janmaat, and Han's (2009) characterisation of a Liberal culture implied that there would be greater access to councils as forums for individual expression and choice. The data appear to better support the latter theory: with 84.3% of schools in these countries having a council, their access levels are above the EU average. Additionally, the similar access levels in England and Ireland appears to support the theoretical grouping of these countries in the same political culture. The lack of cohesiveness within the Mediterranean and Conservative political cultures may be explained by country-specific circumstances, as was the case for Italy; it would surely be hasty to dismiss the political culture groupings on the basis of school council availability. It would, however, be interesting for future research to explore whether these political cultures are better reflected in other educational approaches to citizenship education.

The expected pattern for eastern European countries was not revealed by the empirical analysis. Rather than reduced levels of access in eastern Europe, it would appear that school councils are very common in schools there and at least in line with other European countries. Most strikingly, 100% of Polish schools in the sample appear to have a school council. It seems that Kitanova's (2019) expectation that newer democracies will be less democratic may be mistaken: eastern European countries do not appear to be less democratic in their schools. Our findings align with other research, which associates recent or less stable democracies with *higher* levels of public engagement. Haste (2004) argues that people in new democracies, particularly ex-Soviet countries, may be more engaged as they have more recently experienced great political change. This may have led to increased feelings of political self-efficacy as they have the impression that change is possible. Additionally, she argues that people may feel more idealistic and optimistic about the future in recent democracies, as there is the sense of having a fresh start. This argument seems to accord with a developmental perspective of political engagement, whereby increased feelings of self-efficacy and motivation are thought to lead to increased engagement (e.g. Torney-Purta, Barber, & Wilkenfeld, 2007). That is, in the case of the ex-Soviet countries, engagement may be more influenced by personal feelings than macro-social factors such as age of democracy. There is empirical evidence in the educational context that Haste (2004) may be correct: Antonowicz, Pinheiro, and Smużewska (2014) identified a sharp rise in student representation in Poland between 1989 and 1995. Thus our results seem to align with previous research on the prevalence of democratic practices in newer democracies.

3 The Influence of School Type

As for the school types that are associated with having a council, the initial logistic regression suggested that schools with higher SES composition have a higher predicted probability of having student representation. This appears to support hypothesis 4, which was based on research suggesting that schools with students from more advantaged backgrounds provide a broader curriculum, including more opportunities for political development and engagement (Bischoff, 2016), while disadvantaged student bodies may be subjected to a more narrow focus on academic development and therefore fewer opportunities such as a council (McFarland & Starmanns, 2009).

However, the results of the EU-wide MLA (Table 5) showed a negative association between a school's SES composition and individuals' participation on councils. Alongside this, an individual's SES is associated with *increased* participation. Campbell (2006) explains that a positive association at the individual level, alongside a negative association at the level of the social environment which is *stronger* than the effect of individual SES, provides support for the positional theory of education. Our results provide some support for this theory, as the combination of a negative effect of school SES composition and a positive effect of individual SES is noted in the EU-wide model and Latvia and the Netherlands. This would suggest that, in a social environment where students are, on average, of higher SES, an individual with a given SES participates less. This is because it is those who are of the highest SES *in their environment* who tend to participate more. Marsh et al. (2008) have used the phrase 'big fish, little pond' to describe the same effect in relation to academic self-concept. This phrase reinforces the idea that the social environment may be an important factor in determining the outcome of competitive phenomena. Our results suggest somewhat that this applies to the relationship between SES and school council participation in some countries in the EU. However, since the effect size of individual SES is consistently greater, it still seems an individual's SES has an absolute effect on participation.

Alongside this finding, Table 6 shows that the positional effect is *not* seen in every country in Europe. The country-specific patterns may speak to enduring historic differences in school systems in the EU. For instance, the data presented here suggest that, in England, school SES composition has an important, *positive* effect on council participation, while ethnic composition has a negative association. These findings suggest that school composition in England influences participation such that individuals in socially privileged and ethnic majority schools participate more. This aligns with Maxwell and Aggleton's (2016) claim that England's history of elite schooling has an enduring influence on education today. These authors describe a highly differentiated educational landscape, with a wide range of schooling types. This culture has also recently manifested in the marketisation of education in England, characterised by education that is independent from government combined with the ability of parents to choose their child's school (Hicks, 2015). Indeed, this schooling structure is thought to be an aspect of England's liberal political culture highlighted in this study (Vincent, 2019; Lynch, 2006). Our results signal a country in which differentiated curricula and experiences on the basis of school type are prevalent. On the basis of this study, one might ask whether England's supposedly comprehensive school system is really so, or whether it remains as divided as it has been historically.

The situation in England can be contrasted with Finland, where school SES and ethnic composition have no statistically significant effect on council participation. This aligns with literature on schooling in Finland which highlights how its egalitarian structure, particularly its comprehensive system, means that educational outcomes depend much less on the specific school attended

(Modin et al., 2014). It is thought that the all-through structure of Finnish schools – with no break between primary and secondary school – discourages pupil movement and parent choice at this stage of schooling, creating schools less segregated by SES and ethnicity (Wiborg, 2004). The data presented here may add to this characterisation of Finland's school system as comprehensive and equal: our results suggest that opportunities to participate on the council do not depend on school type. Thus it would appear that historic differences in education systems, influenced by political culture, may still be relevant to the debate on political education today.

On the other hand, the lack of statistical significance with regards to the private school predictor – across the EU (Table 5) as well as in individual countries (Table 6) – may initially be taken as a positive outcome for social justice. It would appear that the Singapore-style differentiation of citizenship education (Ho, 2012) is not replicated in Europe, at least not between private and public schools. If elite schools do indeed develop distinct skills and personality traits, such as self-assurance (Khan, 2011), they do not appear to be doing so through the school council. However, with Whitty and Wisby (2007b), one must still question what qualitative differences might exist between councils at public and private schools. This is especially important given the potential for negative outcomes from tokenistic or powerless councils which undermine pupils' trust in democracy and feelings of self-efficacy (Whitty & Wisby, 2007b; Cross, Hulme, & McKinney, 2014; Alderson, 2000). However, our analysis focused neither on qualitative differences between councils, nor on the subsequent outcomes; we suggest only that quantitative equality of access between public and private schools is a starting point, but unlikely to be the end point.

4 The Influence of Socio-Demographic Characteristics

With regards to the individual characteristics that influence participation on school councils, the results showed a pattern of inequality on the basis of socio-demographic characteristics. The two predictors of participation that stand out as consistently relevant are the pupil's SES and expected level of education. In every analysis, a large, positive and highly statistically significant association is apparent. This result was anticipated by the literature discussed and supports hypotheses 6 and 8, which emerged from that literature. The literature discussed revealed that this is likely to be linked to inherited political disadvantage, whereby children of working-class families may not develop the skills, identities or aspirations that are associated with political participation (e.g. Hoskins & Janmaat, 2019). Our analysis suggests that these same inequalities are manifested in differential access to school councils. This may be due to the selection process for candidates used at most schools: either the candidate is voted for by their peers, or else the teacher selects the candidate (Taylor & Johnson, 2002). In either case, those pupils who are *perceived* to be suitable are likely to win the vote; those pupils who *already* have an interest are likely to put themselves forward. Returning to the developmental approach to political participation, we suggest that these are the students who already have the capabilities (McCowan & Unterhalter, 2013) or identity (Youniss, McLellan, & Yates, 1997) needed to participate. The implications of this finding are discussed below.

It is worth drawing attention again to the bivariate association between expected education and council participation (Figure 5). While an overall positive correlation is apparent, the curious dip in the middle suggests that those who expect a middling amount of education participate on councils the least. Does this indicate a random pattern? We would argue that it does not. Rather, it aligns with previous research that has found an excluded middle in political activities at school (Whitty & Wisby, 2007b). This refers to a group of children who are neither highly motivated nor falling behind. While pupils in the former group may put themselves forward for voluntary activities, pupils in the latter group may be encouraged by teachers who identify the value in such opportunities (ibid.). Indeed, Taylor and Johnson (2002) observe that children exhibiting challenging behaviour are sometimes encouraged to join the school council and, in some cases, this responsibility leads to an improvement in behaviour. The middle group, on the other hand, may be excluded because such pupils neither push themselves, nor are they pushed. This is a pattern that is likely to be particular to schools: in the wider world, there is no-one there to push the least motivated. Thus this explanation aligns with the developmental perspective outlined by the literature on political engagement, but adds the extra dimension of teacher influence. We therefore identify a school-specific group in danger of exclusion: those of middling aspirations. This may also explain why the bivariate association between SES and participation – as shown in Figure 5 – is less consistent for those of low SES. Teacher encouragement may be a confounding third factor in this pattern for those of low SES, leading to a great deal of variation in participation levels for such students, and more consistently high participation rates for those of high SES.

We suggest that the developmental perspective might also be useful in understanding the gender balance of school councils. While the data suggest girls and boys have fairly similar levels of participation, there is still the persistent and statistically significant result that girls participate slightly more. Both sides of this finding deserve some discussion. The similar levels of participation amongst both girls and boys may be explained by research which suggests teachers are increasingly undergoing training on gender equality in schools and aware of such issues (e.g. in the Nordic context, see Cardona López et al., 2018; for Estonia, see Mägi et al., 2016). The school council may be an easy and visible way to implement this training in practice. Equally, as Taylor and Johnson (2002) note, many schools require a representative from each gender for each class.

Yet it is interesting that some small inequality persists in spite of these structural measures to assure equality. The slightly higher participation rate of girls conflicts with Hoskins, Janmaat, and Melis' (2017) speculation that boys may prefer to engage with combative political experiences, such as a council. Moreover, the wider literature on political participation suggests women may participate less (Barrett, 2012). Why, then, do girls seem to participate on councils more? A report from the Organisation for Economic Co-operation and Development (OECD, 2015) on gender in education highlights the continued manifestations of gender inequality in schools. In particular, it is noted that pupils appear to internalise gendered behaviours apparent in society: 'Boys adopt a concept of masculinity that includes a disregard for authority, academic work and formal achievement' (p. 51). Given that participating on the school council is a formal position of some authority and may indicate a commitment to, and interest in, the school, it could be that boys are more reluctant to participate on these grounds. In other words, boys may exclude such formal participation channels from the male identity. Alternatively, girls may display those behaviours and attitudes that make them appear to be ideal candidates for the council (OECD, 2015). In either case, it seems plausible that prior development and self-identification may have a part to play in explaining the small gender disparity in participation levels.

As for ethnicity, its influence appears to depend on the school the individual attends, shown by the significant interaction effect in Model 4, Table 5. Ethnic minority pupils appear to participate less on average (Model 3), but this effect is also compounded and increased by attending a school with many ethnic minority pupils. This would suggest that it is important to consider how ethnicity interacts with the social environment in order to work towards equal access for all. This aligns with Youdell's (2003) research which highlights the relationship between ethnic minority pupils' disadvantage and school culture. While a high ethnic minority composition is associated with lower participation rates for ethnic majority students, this effect is even stronger for ethnic minority students. Drawing on Youdell, it may be that ethnic minority pupils are not perceived as ideal learners and representatives and ethnic majority pupils may be perceived as more suitable for a role on the school council. It is plausible that this is because they appear to resemble more closely the role models who take part in national politics, who tend to be from an ethnic majority (Barreto, 2010). Thus it seems important to consider carefully how the school environment may reflect and reproduce norms found in wider society concerning who is an appropriate candidate for political participation.

The significance of the interaction between SES and ethnicity emphasises the point that multiple and complex identities must be recognised if equitable access to school councils is desired. This is a helpful finding in response to literature which predicts such an interaction but called for more empirical research on the topic (e.g. McCowan & Unterhalter, 2013; Hoskins & Janmaat, 2019). Having found evidence in our empirical research that pupils' sociodemographic characteristics, as well as their intersections, influence access to school councils, we must now ask: What are the theoretical and practical implications of this finding?

5 The Implications of Our Findings

If school councils are to successfully promote space and participation for all – now or in the future – then they must serve to level the playing field for different students. That is, they must provide a space for those who would otherwise be disengaged. Hoskins, Janmaat, and Melis (2017) distinguish between accelerating and mitigating effects with regards to citizenship education at school. If an intervention has an accelerating effect, it promotes and amplifies the voice and skills of those who are already ahead, while a mitigating effect reduces the impact of the initial disadvantage and therefore helps to narrow the gap between the level of political participation of different groups. This is a helpful distinction to use in trying to understand the implications of differential school council access. The developmental perspective highlights that those who already have the skills and identity to participate do so more. As Onken and Lange (2014, p. 71) write, 'When it comes to civic education it seems that students who do not need it look for it, while those who need it try to avoid it'. Our results provide good evidence that this is true of school councils. From a pedagogical perspective, this surely serves to further develop the skills of those who are already ahead, while leaving those who lack the skills further behind. This is particularly pertinent for 13- and 14-year-old pupils since it has been shown that the gap in political engagement widens at the greatest rate at this age (Janmaat & Hoskins, 2021). Moreover, if the snowball effect of participation is correct – where participation engenders further participation – this gap is only likely to widen further (Hoskins, Janmaat, & Melis, 2017; Barrett,

2012). Our analysis would therefore suggest that school councils may have an accelerating effect on the political participation of more advantaged students as opposed to a mitigating effect on disadvantage.

From a normative perspective, differential access raises serious concerns that participation in decision-making at school may be reserved for the elite (Hanafin & Lynch, 2002). In relation to parent voice, it has been observed that participation is rarely representative, as those with more capability and resources are able to shape the conversation (Martin & Vincent, 1999). It seems plausible that the school council, too, may serve as a decision-making platform for students who already hold more power. It is for this reason that some have argued that democratic initiatives are likely to exacerbate unequal power dynamics if they 'fail to bridge deep-seated power differences' (Kirshner & Jefferson, 2015, p. 9). This can be further understood in light of McCowan and Unterhalter's (2013) capability theory, which stresses the importance of recognising difference and diversity within conceptions of the citizen. As these authors write,

> Homogenising forms of citizenship are dangerous in that they can suppress forms of difference that may be valued by the individuals or groups in question, but also because they may ignore disparities in people's ability to exercise the formal rights granted to them. (p. 139)

The interaction between SES and ethnicity indicates the complexity of the effect of intersecting identities on engagement. If schools do not recognise this heterogeneity, there is a risk that a broad-brush approach to citizenship in schools will result in the reproduction of political inequalities. In summary, democracy in which there is only equality of opportunity does not assure real inclusivity; it will not address European Youth Goal 9.

Furthermore, the literature on political identity formation emphasises adolescence as a crucial time, with effects lasting to adulthood (Hoare, 2013; Kahne, Crow, & Lee, 2013; Flanagan, Beyers, & Žukauskienė, 2012). If pupils are excluded from political participation aged 13, this negative (in the sense of absent) experience could be formative. They will not merely be missing out on the positive experience, but also actively experiencing exclusion. Such exclusion may further entrench a disengaged identity as a pupil confirms her self-identification as someone who does not participate. Indeed, this is even more likely in light of the literature on socialisation, which is characterised as unintentional and unconscious learning (Schugurensky, 2006). If knowledge is constructed in the way explored in Chapter 2's literature review, excluded pupils may construct the knowledge that people like them do not participate, and that there is no space for them in politics. Given the importance of role models in identity construction (Haste, 2004), the diversity of a council – in terms of SES, ethnicity, academic potential and gender – should surely be a priority for schools.

It remains to be said that our analyses find clear patterns, but also leave much of the variance to be explained. Indeed, the explained variance of each model is only very small. This indicates that there are other determinants of access to school council which have not been included in our model at the school and individual-levels. This could be due to a range of factors. For instance, at the school-level, some research highlights the unevenness of teacher training in citizenship education (Kerr & Cleaver, 2004) and staff confidence in implementing citizenship education (Weinberg & Flinders, 2018): it may be that the existence of a council at a school is to some extent at the mercy of staffing. This raises the concerning possibility that quality of citizenship provision in schools is not assured, but determined by circumstances. Such randomness may be of concern to those hoping to achieve European Youth Goal 9.

It is likely that much variation at the individual-level can be explained by the personal characteristics of pupils. We suspect that children who are confident, articulate, mature and popular are likely to participate on school councils to a much greater extent than their quieter peers. The patterns discovered in our analysis have been explained on a theoretical level by reference to capabilities and early socialisation. Yet children may develop the characteristics that make them desirable representatives on the school council without such experiences, and children from any social background can have those experiences. That is, pupils of low SES, in minority ethnic groups and with low educational aspirations may have the characteristics that their more advantaged peers are merely more *likely* to have. In such a case, we would imagine that disadvantaged pupils are just as likely to participate on the school council. We would therefore expect a similar study using personality predictors to explain much more of the variance than our analysis.

Yet this would really have constituted a different kind of study, in any case. Our research has examined the role of school councils in addressing or perpetuating political inequalities. These inequalities might be considered structural when there are distinct patterns amongst groups with certain characteristics, whereby some groups face barriers to participation that others do not (Bramesfeld & Good, 2016). Schools could make changes to ensure pupils with all personalities are able to access councils. However, education will surely contribute to more systemic and fundamental change if their action is directed at individuals belonging to *groups* who are politically disadvantaged in wider society. It is this persistence of political inequality on the basis of socio-demographic characteristics that leads to institutional and systematic exclusion, as whole groups – and not just individuals – are marginalised from the political sphere.

CHAPTER 7

Improving Democratic Education

Our study took European Youth Goal 9 as its starting point. This supranational goal, formulated by the European Union (2018), speaks to the ideal of political equality for all young people in the EU. The issue of teaching for democracy is complex and we highlighted the tension between developing democratic citizens within an often-authoritarian school context. School councils are one proposed solution to this problem. Therefore, focusing on how school councils may address European Youth Goal 9, we described how they have been justified in the literature on pedagogical and normative grounds. After having established that school councils may contribute to meeting the goal, we examined issues around access to participation. We approached the question of access from three levels: national, school and individual. From the literature on varieties of democracy in Europe emerged the hypothesis that there would be differential access to school councils based on political culture. The literature at the school level indicated that there may be uneven access to school councils on the basis of school type. Finally, we reviewed some of the literature on barriers to political participation – both in society and in school – on the basis of socio-demographic characteristics. We used the developmental perspective to elucidate how differences in levels of participation may be due to the identity and capability of the individual. We argued that this would still constitute a barrier to participation, but a barrier that stems from the person, rather than external circumstances.

Moving into the empirical part of the study, we therefore conceptualised a barrier to school council participation in two distinct ways: an internal barrier and an external one. To investigate these two kinds of access, we used data from the ICCS and the data analysis programme SPSS. Our quantitative analysis aimed to uncover patterns in uneven access to school councils. To investigate the first kind of access, we examined the proportion of schools within each country and each political culture with a school council. While we found some variation between countries and some evidence of distinct political cultures, we were also struck by the similar levels of access in many countries across the EU. In the discussion, we suggested that converging policies and educational tools may conceal genuine differences in political cultures. As the world apparently converges with supranational organisations (such as the EU) increasingly setting goals, it is interesting to question the extent to which convergence of policies truly indicates convergence of cultures. To investigate the role of school type in determining access to school councils, we conducted a logistic regression analysis to discover what kinds of schools are most likely to have a council. We found that private schools seem no more likely to have a council than public schools; this result was then supported by multi-level analysis (MLA). The influence of SES and ethnic composition proved to be slightly more complex and country-dependent. The MLA included explanatory variables at the individual, school and national-levels and aimed to discover what factors are associated with increased participation amongst individuals. The results suggested that socio-demographic factors influence access to school councils. Moreover, the influence of these factors was found to interact with the characteristics of the school the individual attended.

Worryingly, we found that SES and expected years of further education had the strongest effects on participation in a school council in established democracies such as England and the Netherlands. Thus, decades of democratic rule in these countries have not been able to reduce pronounced social inequality in access to school councils as key breeding grounds for active citizenship. In this respect, school practice in these countries remains far away from the ideal of equal participation. Future research would need to examine closely what exclusionary processes are happening in the schools in these countries deterring children from disadvantaged backgrounds to put themselves forward for election to the school council.

The title of this book asks whether school councils are democratic forums or exclusive clubs. Our results suggest strongly that they may be the latter. While councils might have the potential to address European Youth Goal 9, it would appear that much more attention needs to be paid to who benefits from them. From both a pedagogical and normative perspective, there is a risk that councils – with access in its current state – may amplify the voices of the politically privileged and silence the rest. This has implications beyond the school as there is strong evidence that the political identity and dispositions formed in adolescence endure through adulthood (Youniss, McLellan, & Yates, 1997; Keating & Janmaat, 2016; Janmaat & Hoskins, 2021). Access issues to school councils may contribute to the political marginalisation of some groups. If this is the case, then schools would appear to be a tool for maintaining the status quo, as opposed to tools for social change in this sphere. Previously, there has been research on the efficacy of school councils and the implications of powerless or tokenistic councils (e.g. Whitty & Wisby, 2007b; Schugurensky, 2006). We hope to have added to the literature by highlighting the potential consequences of differential *access*.

Going forward, we would recommend that schools carefully review the selection or election process for representatives on the school council. There appears to have been some success in ensuring near gender equality. Schools should now think about how to promote other forms of diversity amongst its student representatives, notably by fostering the participation of children of disadvantaged backgrounds. This may require more than a quota specifying, for instance, a certain number of students on free school meals (as a much used indicator of social disadvantage in the United Kingdom) in the council. Rather, we would suggest that school councils are not used as stand-alone initiatives relying on previously acquired skills, but combined with programmes which aim to develop the skills and political identity of all students in a comprehensive way.

The role of teachers cannot be underestimated here. Teachers can disrupt the invisible and creeping marginalisation of students of disadvantaged backgrounds by closely monitoring and actively encouraging their participation in a whole range of civic learning opportunities, not just school councils. By supporting pupils to develop those civic competences highlighted in Chapter 2, teachers will be equipping them for participation on the school council as well as participation in future democratic life. Teachers – in any subject or role – can support the development of civic competences in many ways. For instance, they could encourage pupils to take on leadership roles, take the initiative in organising events and campaigns, chair meetings and put topics on the agenda for classroom discussions.

Such strategies will often need to counteract or even constrain the *voluntary nature* of participation in such opportunities as it is this optional character that leads to the overrepresentation of children from middle class backgrounds in these activities (Hoskins & Janmaat, 2019). Take the example of a classroom discussion. The teacher could employ a range of strategies to promote more equal participation, ranging from light-touch to interventionist. On the light-touch end, the teacher could scaffold discussions with sentence prompts or cue cards so that quieter children feel supported to speak up. They may structure discussions so that all pupils are prompted to speak, for example by assigning different roles to pupils. On the more interventionist end, it might be helpful for teachers to call specifically on those who speak less rather than leaving it up to children to regulate their own participation. When groups are created to discuss political issues and representatives are chosen to report the group discussion back to the whole class, the teacher can give turns in selecting the representatives. In other words, ensuring more equal participation requires a more active and possibly interventionist role of the teacher.

If representation in school councils is pursued as part of this more encompassing set of practices to attain equal access, school councils may move away from their current status as exclusive clubs, and towards becoming a true democratic forum. This would surely be a positive starting point on the journey towards political equality.

APPENDIX

Full Wording and Coding from the ICCS Questionnaires for All Applicable Variables

Variable	Questionnaire	Question	Complete wording	Possible responses	Our coding
Does the school have a school council? (DV1)	School	7a	How many (target grade) students in this school elect their class representatives?	(1) All or nearly all; (2) Most of them; (3) Some of them; (4) None or hardly any; (5) Not applicable	1, 2, 3 = 1; 4, 5 = 0
Have you participated on a school council? (DV2)	Student	15f	At school, have you ever done any of the following activities? Please think about all schools you have been enrolled at since the first year of (ISCED level 1). Becoming a candidate for (class representative) or (school parliament).	(1) Yes, I have done this within the last twelve months; (2) Yes, I have done this but more than a year ago; (3) No, I have never done this.	1, 2 = 1; 3 = 0

(cont.)

Variable	Questionnaire	Question	Complete wording	Possible responses	Our coding
Public/private school	School	19	Is this school a public or private school?	(1) A public school. This is a school managed directly or indirectly by a public education authority, government agency, or governing board, appointed by government or elected by public franchise. (2) A private school. This is a school managed directly or indirectly by a non-government organisation; for example, a church, trade union, business or other private institution.	1 = 0; 2 = 1
Socio-economic status					
Father's level of education	Student	9	What is the (highest level of education) completed by your father or (male guardian)?	(1) (ISCED level 5A or 6); (2) (ISCED level 4 or 5B); (3) (ISCED level 3); (4) (ISCED level 2); (5) (ISCED level 1); (6) He did not complete (ISCED level 1)	1 = 1; 2 = 2; 3 = 3; 4 = 4; 5 = 5; 6 = 6
Mother's level of education	Student	7	What is the (highest level of education) completed by your mother or (female guardian)?	(1) (ISCED level 5A or 6); (2) (ISCED level 4 or 5B); (3) (ISCED level 3); (4) (ISCED level 2); (5) (ISCED level 1); (6) She did not complete (ISCED level 1)	1 = 1; 2 = 2; 3 = 3; 4 = 4; 5 = 5; 6 = 6

APPENDIX

Variable	Questionnaire	Question	Complete wording	Possible responses	Our coding
Number of books in the home	Student	11	About how many books are there in your home? There are usually about 40 books per metre of shelving. Do not count magazines, newspapers, comic strips or your schoolbooks.	(1) 0–10 books; (2) 11–25 books; (3) 26–100 books; (4) 101–200 books; (5) 201–500 books; (6) More than 500 books	1 = 1; 2 = 2; 3 = 3; 4 = 4; 5 = 5; 6 = 6
Ethnicity	Student	2b	(What best describes you?)	Country dependent.	1 = 1; 2, 3, 4 = 0
Educational aspirations	Student	3	Which of the following (levels of education) do you expect to complete?	(1) (ISCED level 5A or 6); (2) (ISCED level 4 or 5B); (3) (ISCED level 3); (4) (ISCED level 2); (5) I do not expect to complete (ISCED level 2)	1 = 1; 2 = 2; 3 = 3; 4 = 4; 5 = 5
Gender	Student	2	Are you a girl or a boy?	(1) girl; (2) boy	1 = 0; 2 = 1

References

Abrams, F. (2017, December 5). 'Drill and kill'? English schools turn to scripted lessons to raise standards. *The Guardian*. https://www.theguardian.com/education/2017/dec/05/drill-english-schools-scripted-lessons-raise-standards-michaela

Adams, R. (2016, December 30). 'No excuses': Inside Britain's strictest school. *The Guardian*. https://www.theguardian.com/education/2016/dec/30/no-excuses-inside-britains-strictest-school

Adan, T. (2018). *Political participation of refugees: The case of Syrian and Somali refugees in Sweden*. International Institute for Democracy and Electoral Assistance.

Aggleton, P., & Maxwell, C. (Eds.). (2016). *Elite education: International perspectives*. Routledge.

Ainley, J., Schulz, W., & Friedman, T. (Eds.). (2013). *ICCS 2009 Encyclopedia: Approaches to civic and citizenship education around the world*. IEA. Retrieved May 29, 2020, from https://www.iea.nl/sites/default/files/2019-04/ICCS_2009_Encyclopedia.pdf

Alderson, P. (2000). School students' views on school councils and daily life at school. *Children and Society, 14*(2), 121–134.

Allman, P. (2010). *Critical education against global capitalism: Karl Marx and revolutionary critical education*. Brill.

Almond, G., & Verba, S. (1963). *The civic culture: Political attitudes and democracy in 5 nations*. Princeton University Press.

Amnå, E. (2012). How is civic engagement developed over time? Emerging answers from a multidisciplinary field. *Journal of Adolescence, 35*(3), 611–627.

Anderson, J. R., Reder, L. M., & Simon, H. A. (1996). Situated learning and education. *Educational Researcher, 25*(4), 5–11.

Angell, A. V. (1998). Practicing democracy at school: A qualitative analysis of an elementary class council. *Theory and Research in Social Education, 26*(2), 149–172.

Antonowicz, D., Pinheiro, R., & Smużewska, M. (2014). The changing role of students' representation in Poland: An historical appraisal. *Studies in Higher Education, 39*(3), 470–484.

Arnhem Wharf Primary School. (2022). *School council*. Retrieved June 10, 2022, from https://www.arnhemwharfprimaryschool.com/School-Council/

Barlows Primary School. (2022). *School council visit to London*. Retrieved June 10, 2022, from https://barlowsprimary.co.uk/news/london-visit/

Barreto, M. (2010). *Ethnic cues: The role of shared ethnicity in Latino political participation*. University of Michigan Press.

Barrett, M. (2012). *The PIDOP Project: An overview*. Retrieved May 15, 2020, from http://epubs.surrey.ac.uk/775796/1/Barrett%20(2012).pdf

REFERENCES

Bennett, L. W., Wells, C., & Freelon, D. (2011). Communicating civic engagement: Contrasting models of citizenship in the youth web sphere. *Journal of Communication, 61*(5), 835–856.

Bennett, T. (2012, March 12). School councils: Shut up, we're listening. *The Guardian.* https://www.theguardian.com/education/2012/mar/12/school-councils-number-lip-service

Bischoff, K. (2016). The civic effects of schools: Theory and empirics. *Theory and Research in Education, 14*(1), 91–106.

Bowles, S., & Gintis, H. (1976). *Schooling in capitalist America: Educational reform and the contradictions of economic life.* Basic Books.

Brady, H. E., Schlozman, K. L., & Verba, S. (2015). Political mobility and political reproduction from generation to generation. *The Annals of the American Academy of Political and Social Science, 657*(1), 149–173.

Bramesfeld, K. D., & Good, A. (2016). C'est la vie! The game of social life: Using an intersectionality approach to teach about privilege and structural inequality. *Teaching of Psychology, 43*(4), 294–304.

Breen, R., & Müller, W. (2020). *Education and intergenerational social mobility in Europe and the United States.* Stanford University Press.

Brese, F., Jung, M., Mirazchiyski, P., Schulz, W., & Zuehlke, O. (2011). *ICCS 2009 user guide for the international database.* IEA. Retrieved May 29, 2020, from https://www.iea.nl/sites/default/files/2019-04/ICCS_2009_IDB_User_Guide.pdf

Burnitt, M., & Gunter, H. (2013). Primary school councils: Organization, composition and head teacher perceptions and values. *Management in Education, 27*(2), 56–62.

Burns, N., Verba, S., & Schlozman, K. (2003). Unequal at the starting line: Creating participatory inequalities across generations and among groups. *The American Sociologist, 34*(1–2), 45–69.

Campbell, D. (2006). What is education's impact on civic and social engagement? In R. Desjardins & T. Schuller (Eds.), *Measuring the effects of education on health and civic engagement: Proceedings of the Copenhagen symposium* (pp. 25–126). Organisation for Economic Co-operation and Development. Retrieved August 21, 2020, from http://www.oecd.org/education/innovation-education/37437718.pdf

Campbell, D. (2007). Sticking together: Classroom diversity and civic education. *American Politics Research, 35*(1), 57–78.

Campbell, D. (2008). Voice in the classroom: How an open classroom climate fosters political engagement among adolescents. *Political Behavior, 30*(4), 437–454.

Cardona López, J. A., Nordfjell, O. B., Gaini, F., & Heikkinen, M. (2018). Promising Nordic practices in gender equality promotion: Developing teacher education dialogue, practice, and policy cycles on-line. *Policy Futures in Education, 16*(5), 605–619.

Castagno, A. (2008). Improving academic achievement, But at what cost? The demands of diversity and equity at Birch Middle School. *Journal of Cases in Educational Leadership, 11*, 1–9.

Catarci, M. (2018). Citizenship education from an intercultural perspective: Theories, approaches and practices in the Italian context. In N. Palaiologou & M. Zembylas (Eds.), *Human rights and citizenship education: An intercultural perspective* (pp. 237–257). Cambridge Scholars Publishing.

Cotmore, R. (2004). Organisational competence: The study of a school council in action. *Children & Society, 18*(1), 53–65.

Council of Europe. (2015). *Revised European charter on the participation of young people in local and regional life*. Retrieved May 15, 2020, from https://rm.coe.int/168071b4d6

Council of Europe. (2016). *Factsheet on the framework convention for the protection of national minorities*. Retrieved July 10, 2022, from https://www.coe.int/en/web/minorities/fcnm-factsheet

Council of Europe. (2020). *Participation*. Retrieved May 15, 2020, from https://pjp-eu.coe.int/en/web/youth-partnership/participation

Cox, S., & Robinson-Pant, A. (2005). Challenging perceptions of school councils in the primary school. *Education 3–13, 33*(2), 14–19.

Cross, B., Hulme, M., & McKinney, S. (2014). The last place to look: the place of school councils within citizen participation in Scottish schools. *Oxford Review of Education, 40*(5), 628–648.

de Boer, H., & Stensaker, B. (2007). An internal representative system: The democratic vision. In P. Maassen & J. P. Olsen (Eds.), *University dynamics and European integration* (pp. 99–118). Springer Netherlands.

Dewey, J. (1954). *Democracy and education*. Macmillan Company.

Dubet, F. (2013). Social cohesion as paradigm. In J. G. Janmaat, M. Duru-Bellat, A. Green, & P. Méhaut (Eds.), *The dynamics and social outcomes of education systems* (pp. 141–159). Palgrave Macmillan.

Eckstein, K., Noack, P., & Gniewosz, B. (2012). Attitudes toward political engagement and willingness to participate in politics: Trajectories throughout adolescence. *Journal of Adolescence, 35*(3), 485–495.

Erikson, E. (1968). *Identity, youth and crisis*. Faber and Faber.

Esping Andersen, G. (1990). *The three worlds of welfare capitalism*. Polity.

European Commission. (2009). *EU youth report*. Retrieved May 15, 2020, from https://pjp-eu.coe.int/documents/42128013/47261653/youth_report_final.pdf/93e126eb-a18c-4864-ba67-0c0ffad361db

European Commission. (2017). *Citizenship education at school in Europe – 2017. Eurydice report*. Publications Office of the European Union.

European Network against Racism. (2019). *ENAR's election analysis – Ethnic minorities in the new European Parliament 2019–2025*. Retrieved July 10, 2022, from https://www.enar-eu.org/enar-s-election-analysis-ethnic-minorities-in-the-new-european-parliament-2019/

REFERENCES

European Union. (2018). *Official Journal of the European Union, C 456*. Retrieved May 15, 2020, from https://eur-lex.europa.eu/legal-content/EN/TXT/PDF/?uri=OJ:C:2018:456:FULL&from=EN

European Union News. (2021). *School council pupils question councillors on local environmental issues*. Retrieved June 10, 2022, from https://link.gale.com/apps/doc/A679610947/ITOF?u=ucl_ttda&sid=bookmark-ITOF&xid=236035e7

Ferreira, P. D., Azevedo, C. N., & Menezes, I. (2012). The developmental quality of participation experiences: Beyond the rhetoric that "participation is always good!" *Journal of Adolescence, 35*(3), 599–610.

Finkel, S. E., & Ernst, H. R. (2005). Civic education in post-apartheid South Africa: Alternative paths to the development of political knowledge and democratic values. *Political Psychology, 26*, 333–364.

Flanagan, C., Beyers, W., & Žukauskienė, R. (2012). Political and civic engagement development in adolescence. *Journal of Adolescence, 35*(3), 471–473.

Flemmen, M. (2016). Elite education and class reproduction. In P. Aggleton & C. Maxwell (Eds.), *Elite education: International perspectives* (pp. 126–131). Routledge.

Fraga, B. (2018). *The turnout gap: Race, ethnicity, and political inequality in a diversifying America*. Cambridge University Press.

Freire, P. (1970). *Pedagogy of the oppressed*. Penguin Books Ltd.

Fuchs, D., & Klingemann, H. (2006). Democratic communities in Europe: A comparison between East and West. In D. Fuchs, H. Klingemann, & J. Zielonka (Eds.), *Democracy and political culture in Eastern Europe* (pp. 25–66). Routledge.

Garson, G. (2013). Preparing to analyze multilevel data. In G. Garson (Ed.), *Hierarchical linear modeling: Guide and applications* (pp. 27–54). Sage.

Gear, J., McIntosh, A., & Squires, G. (1994). *Informal learning in the professions*. Department of Adult Education, University of Hull.

Geboers, E., Geijsel, F., Admiraal, W., & Ten Dam, G. (2013). Review of the effects of citizenship education. *Educational Research Review, 9*, 158–173.

Gillborn, D. (1990). *'Race' ethnicity and education: Teaching and learning in multi-ethnic schools*. Unwin Hyman.

Great Britain. Department for Education. (2017). *Unlocking talent, fulfilling potential: A plan for improving social mobility through education*. Retrieved May 15, 2020, from https://assets.publishing.service.gov.uk/government/uploads/system/uploads/attachment_data/file/667690/Social_Mobility_Action_Plan_-_for_printing.pdf

Green, A., Janmaat, J. G., & Han, C. (2009). *Regimes of social cohesion*. Centre for Learning and Life Chances in Knowledge Economies and Societies.

Hahn, C. (1998). *Becoming political: Comparative perspectives on citizenship education*. State University of New York Press.

Han, C., Janmaat, J. G., May, T., & Morris, P. (2013). Curriculum patterns in citizenship education. In J. G. Janmaat, M. Duru-Bellat, A. Green, & P. Mehaut (Eds.), *The dynamics and social outcomes of education systems* (pp. 116–138). Palgrave Macmillan.

Hanafin, J., & Lynch, A. (2002). Peripheral voices: Parental involvement, social class, and educational disadvantage. *British Journal of Sociology of Education, 23*(1), 35–49.

Haraldstad, Å., Tveit, A. D., & Kovač, V. B. (2022). Democracy in schools: Qualitative analysis of pupils' experiences of democracy in the context of the Norwegian school. *Cambridge Journal of Education, 52*(1), 73–89.

Hart, R. A. (1992). *Children's participation: From tokenism to citizenship*. UNICEF. Retrieved May 15, 2020, from https://www.unicef-irc.org/publications/pdf/childrens_participation.pdf

Haste, H. (2004). Constructing the citizen. *Political Psychology, 25*(3), 413–439.

Heath, A. F., Fisher, S. D., Rosenblatt, G., Sanders, D., & Sobolewska, M. (2013). *The political integration of ethnic minorities in Britain*. Oxford University Press.

Heck, R., Thomas, S., & Tabata, L. (2014). *Multilevel and longitudinal modeling with IBM SPSS* (2nd ed.). Routledge.

Helgøy, I., & Homme, A. (2006). Policy tools and institutional change: Comparing education policies in Norway, Sweden and England. *Journal of Public Policy, 26*(2), 141–165.

Henn, M., & Foard, N. (2014). Social differentiation in young people's political participation: The impact of social and educational factors on youth political engagement in Britain. *Journal of Youth Studies, 17*(3), 360–380.

Hicks, T. (2015). Inequality, marketisation and the left: Schools policy in England and Sweden. *European Journal of Political Research, 54*(2), 326–342.

Ho, L. (2012). Sorting citizens: Differentiated citizenship education in Singapore. *Journal of Curriculum Studies, 44*(3), 403–428.

Hoare, C. (2013). Three missing dimensions in contemporary studies of identity: The unconscious, negative attributes, and society. *Journal of Theoretical and Philosophical Psychology, 33*(1), 51–67.

Hoskins, B., & Janmaat, J. G. (2019). *Education, democracy and inequality: Political engagement and citizenship education in Europe*. Palgrave Macmillan.

Hoskins, B., Janmaat, J. G., & Melis, G. (2017). Tackling inequalities in political socialisation: A systematic analysis of access to and mitigation effects of learning citizenship at school. *Social Science Research, 68*, 88–101.

Hoskins, B., Janmaat, J. G., & Villalba, E. (2012). Learning citizenship through social participation outside and inside school: An international, multilevel study of young people's learning of citizenship. *British Educational Research Journal, 38*(3), 419–446.

IBM Corp. (2017). *IBM SPSS statistics for Macintosh, Version 25.0*. IBM Corp.

Ichilov, O. (2002). Differentiated civics curriculum and patterns of citizenship education: Vocational and academic programs in Israel. In D. Scott & H. Lawson (Eds.),

Citizenship, education, and the curriculum (pp. 88–107). Greenwood Publishing Group.

Janmaat, J. G., & Green, A. (2022). Liberal, republican, conservative and social-democratic mindsets? Exploring the existence of citizenship regimes in civic attitudes. *Social Indicators Research*. Advanced online publication. https://link.springer.com/article/10.1007/s11205-022-02926-5

Janmaat, J. G., & Hoskins, B. (2021). The changing impact of family background on political engagement during adolescence and early adulthood. *Social Forces*. Advanced online publication. https://doi.org/10.1093/sf/soab112

Janner-Raimondi, M. (2015). Formes et pratiques de conseils d'élèves : Quelle(s) responsabilité(s) en jeu ? *Les Sciences de l'éducation – Pour l'Ère nouvelle, 48*, 23–45.

Jennings, M. K. (1979). Another look at the life cycle and political participation. *American Journal of Political Science, 23*(4), 755–71.

Kahne, J., Crow, D., & Lee, N. (2013). Different pedagogy, different politics: High school learning opportunities and youth political engagement. *Political Psychology, 34*(3), 419–441.

Kahne, J., & Middaugh, E. (2008a). *Democracy for some: The civic opportunity gap in high school*. CIRCLE Working Paper 59. Retrieved May 15, 2020, from https://files.eric.ed.gov/fulltext/ED503646.pdf

Kahne, J., & Middaugh, E. (2008b). High quality civic education: What is it and who gets it? *Social Education, 72*(1), 34–39.

Kam, C. D., & Palmer, C. L. (2008). Reconsidering the effects of education on political participation. *The Journal of Politics, 70*(3), 612–631.

Keating, A. (2014). *Education for citizenship in Europe*. Palgrave Macmillan.

Keating, A., & Janmaat, J. G. (2016). Education through citizenship at school: Do school activities have a lasting impact on youth political engagement? *Parliamentary Affairs, 69*(2), 409–429.

Kennedy, K. (2012). Global trends in civic and citizenship education: What are the lessons for Nation States? *Educational Sciences, 2*, 121–135.

Kennedy, M., & Power, M. J. (2008). 'The smokescreen of meritocracy': Elite education in Ireland and the reproduction of class privilege. *Journal for Critical Education Policy Studies, 8*(2), 223–248.

Keogh, A. F., & Whyte, J. (2005). *Second level student councils in Ireland: A study of enablers, barriers and supports*. Stationery Office. Retrieved June 10, 2022, from https://www.tcd.ie/tricc/assets/pdfs/crc-archive/2005-Keogh-Whyte-Student-councils.pdf

Kerr, D. (1999). *Citizenship education: An international comparison*. Retrieved November 30, 2022, from https://www.seameo.org/img/Programmes_Projects/Competition/SEAMEOJapanESD_Award/2013_SEAMEOJapanESD_Award/pub/citizenship_no_intro.pdf

Kerr, D., & Cleaver, E. (2004). *Citizenship education longitudinal study: Literature review – Citizenship education one year on – What does it mean? Emerging definitions and approaches in the first year of national curriculum citizenship in England*. National Foundation for Educational Research. Retrieved August 21, 2020, from https://dera.ioe.ac.uk/5430/1/RR532.pdf

Khan, S. R. (2011). *Privilege: The making of an adolescent elite at St. Paul's school*. Princeton University Press.

Kinder, D. R. (2006). Politics and the life cycle. *Science, 312*(5782), 1905–1908.

Kirshner, B., & Jefferson, A. (2015). Participatory democracy and struggling schools: Making space for youth in school turnarounds. *Teachers College Record, 117*(6), 1–26.

Kitanova, M. (2019). Youth political participation in the EU: Evidence from a cross-national analysis. *Journal of Youth Studies*. https://doi.org/10.1080/13676261.2019.1636951

Klemenčič, M. (2012). Student representation in Western Europe: Introduction to the special issue. *European Journal of Higher Education, 2*(1), 2–19.

Klingemann, H., Fuchs, D., & Zielonka, J. (2006). *Democracy and political culture in Eastern Europe*. Routledge.

Knowles, R. T., Torney-Purta, J., & Barber, C. (2018). Enhancing citizenship learning with international comparative research: Analyses of IEA civic education datasets. *Citizenship Teaching & Learning, 13*(1), 7–30.

Kränzl-Nagl, R., & Zartler, U. (2010). Children's participation in school and community: European perspectives. In B. Percy-Smith & N. Thomas (Eds.), *A handbook of children and young people's participation perspectives from theory and practice* (pp. 164–173). Routledge.

Lee, V. E. (2000). Using hierarchical linear modeling to study social contexts: The case of school effects. *Educational Psychologist, 35*(2), 125–141.

Lerner, R. M., Fisher, C. B., & Weinberg, R. A. (2000). Toward a science for and of the people: Promoting civil society through the application of developmental science. *Child Development, 71*(1), 11–20.

Levinson, M. (2007). *The civic achievement gap*. CIRCLE Working Paper 51. Retrieved May 15, 2020, from http://nrs.harvard.edu/urn-3:HUL.InstRepos:10861134

Lewis-Beck, M. S., Bryman, A., & Liao, T. F. (Eds.). (2004). *The Sage encyclopedia of social science research methods*. Sage Publications.

Lynch, K. (2006). Neo-liberalism and marketisation: The implications for higher education. *European Educational Research Journal, 5*(1), 1–17.

Mager, U., & Nowak, P. (2012). Effects of student participation in decision making at school. A systematic review and synthesis of empirical research. *Educational Research Review, 7*(1), 38–61.

Mägi, E., Biin, H., Trasberg, K., & Kruus, K. (2016). Gender awareness and attitudes toward gender equality among students participating in teacher training. *Estonian Journal of Educational Sciences, 4*(1), 159–194.

REFERENCES

Marsh, H. W., Trautwein, U., Ludtke, O., & Brettschneider, W. (2008). Social comparison and big-fish-little-pond effects on self-concept and other self-belief constructs. *Journal of Educational Psychology, 100*, 510–524.

Martin, J., & Vincent, C. (1999). Parental voice: An exploration. *International Studies in Sociology of Education, 9*(2), 133–154.

Maxwell, C., & Aggleton, P. (2016). Schools, schooling and elite status in English education – changing configurations? *L'Année Sociologique, 66*(1), 147–170.

McCowan, T., & Unterhalter, E. (2013). Education, citizenship and deliberative democracy: Sen's capability perspective. In R. Hedtke & T. Zimenkova (Eds.), *Education for civic and political participation: A critical approach* (pp. 135–154). Routledge.

McDevitt, M., & Kiousis, S. (2006). Deliberative learning: An evaluative approach to interactive civic education. *Communication Education, 55*, 247–264.

McFarland, D. A., & Starmanns, C. (2009). Inside student government: The variable quality of high school student councils. *Teachers College Record, 111*, 27–54.

Medina, M. A., Grim, J., Cosby, G., & Brodnax, R. (2020). The power of community school councils in urban schools. *Peabody Journal of Education, 95*(1), 73–89.

Modin, B., Karvonen, S., Rahkonen, O., & Östberg, V. (2014). School performance, school segregation, and stress-related symptoms: Comparing Helsinki and Stockholm. *School Effectiveness and School Improvement, 26*(3), 467–486.

Mowen, T., & Parker, K. (2017). Minority threat and school security: Assessing the impact of Black and Hispanic student representation on school security measures. *Security Journal, 30*, 504–522.

Nie, N., Junn, J., & Stehlik-Barry, K. (1996). *Education and democratic citizenship in America*. Chicago University Press.

Nussbaum, M. (2000). *Women and human development: The capabilities approach*. Cambridge University Press.

Onken, H., & Lange, D. (2014). Social background, civic education and political participation of young people – The German case. *Journal of Social Science Education, 13*(3), 68–72.

Organisation for Economic Co-operation and Development. (2015). *The ABC of gender equality in education: Aptitude, behaviour, confidence*. PISA, OECD Publishing.

Perry, C. (2011). *School councils*. Northern Ireland Assembly. Retrieved May 15, 2020, from https://dera.ioe.ac.uk/27467/1/8511.pdf

Pharis, T., Bass, R. V., & Pate, J. L. (2018). School council member perceptions and actual practice of school councils in rural schools. *The Rural Educator, 26*(2), 33–38.

Preuss, U., Everson, M., Koenig-Archibugi, M., & Lefebvre, E. (2003). Traditions of citizenship in the European Union. *Citizenship Studies, 7*(1), 3–14.

Quintelier, E., & Hooghe, E. (2013). The relationship between political participation intentions of adolescents and a participatory democratic climate at school in 35 countries. *Oxford Review of Education, 39*(5), 567–89.

Roberts, J. K., Monaco, J., Stovall, H., & Foster, V. (2010). Explained variance in multilevel models. In J. J. Hox & J. K. Roberts (Eds.), *Handbook of advanced multilevel analysis* (pp. 219–230). Routledge.

Rubin, B. (2007). 'There's still not justice': Youth civic identity development amid distinct school and community contexts. *Teachers College Record, 109*(2), 449–481.

Sandovici, M. E., & Listhaug, O. (2010). Ethnic and linguistic minorities and political participation in Europe. *International Journal of Comparative Sociology, 51*(1–2), 111–136.

Schlozman, K. L., Verba, S., & Brady, H. E. (2012). *The unheavenly chorus: Unequal political voice and the broken promise of American democracy.* Princeton University Press.

Schugurensky, D. (2006). "This is our school of citizenship": Informal learning in local democracy. *Counterpoints, 249*, 163–182.

Sen, A. (1980). Equality of what? In S. McMurrin (Ed.), *Tanner lectures on human values* (Vol. 1). Cambridge University Press.

Simovska, V. (2012). Case study of a participatory health-promotion intervention in school. *Democracy & Education, 20*(1).

Taylor, M. J., & Johnson, R. (2002). *School councils: Their role in citizenship and personal and social education.* National Foundation for Educational Research.

Ten Dam, G. T. M., & Volman, M. (2003). Life jacket and the art of living: Social competence and the reproduction of inequality in education. *Curriculum Inquiry, 33*(2), 117–137.

Thornberg, R., & Elvstrand, H. (2012). Children's experiences of democracy, participation, and trust in school. *International Journal of Educational Research, 53*, 44–54.

Torney-Purta, J. (2002). The school's role in developing civic engagement: A study of adolescents in twenty-eight countries. *Applied Developmental Science, 6*, 203–212.

Torney-Purta, J., Barber, C., & Wilkenfeld, B. (2007). Latino adolescents' civic development in the United States: Research results from the IEA Civic Education Study. *Journal of Youth and Adolescents, 36*, 111–125.

Torney-Purta, J., Lehmann, R., Oswald, H., & Schulz, W. (2001). *Citizenship and education in twenty-eight countries: Civic knowledge and engagement at age fourteen.* International Association for the Evaluation in Educational Achievement. Retrieved May 15, 2020, from https://www.iea.nl/sites/default/files/2019-04/CIVED_Phase2_Age_Fourteen.pdf

Uberoi, E., & Johnston, N. (2021). *Political disengagement in the UK: Who is disengaged?* House of Commons Library. Retrieved July 10, 2022, from https://researchbriefings.files.parliament.uk/documents/CBP-7501/CBP-7501.pdf

US Census Bureau. (2021). *Voting rates by race and Hispanic origin.* Retrieved August 9, 2022, from https://www.census.gov/library/visualizations/2017/comm/voting-rates-race-hispanic.html

van de Werfhorst, H. G. (2009). *Education, inequality and active citizenship: Tensions in a differentiated schooling system*. AIAS Working Paper 09-73. Retrieved November 29, 2022, from https://aias.s3-eu-central-1.amazonaws.com/website/uploads/1456775026037WP73.pdf

Verba, S. (2003). Would the dream of political equality turn out to be a nightmare? *Perspectives on Politics, 1*(4), 663–679.

Verba, S., Scholzman, K. L., & Brady, H. E. (1995). *Voice and equality: Civic volunteerism in American politics*. Harvard University Press.

Vincent, C. (2019). *Tea and the queen? Fundamental British values, education and citizenship*. Policy Press.

Walther, A. (2012). Learning to participate or participating to learn? In P. Loncle, M. Cuconato, V. Muniglia, & A. Walther (Eds.), *Youth participation in Europe: Beyond discourses, practices and realities* (pp. 189–206). Bristol University Press.

Weinberg, J., & Flinders, M. (2018). Learning for democracy: The politics and practice of citizenship education. *British Educational Research Journal, 44*(4), 573–592.

Westheimer, J., & Kahne, J. (2004). What kind of citizen? The politics of educating for democracy. *American Educational Research Journal, 41*(2), 237–269.

Whitty, G., & Wisby, E. (2007a). *Real decision making? School councils in action*. Research report DCSF-RR001. Department for Children, Schools and Families.

Whitty, G., & Wisby, E. (2007b). Whose voice? An exploration of the current policy interest in pupil involvement in school decision-making. *International Studies in Sociology of Education, 17*(3), 303–319.

Wiborg, S. (2004) Education and social integration: A comparative study of the comprehensive school system in Scandinavia. *London Review of Education, 2*(2), 83–93.

Wilensky, H. (2002). *Rich democracies: Political economy, public policy, and performance*. University of California Press.

Wyness, M. (2009). Children representing children: Participation and the problem of diversity in UK youth councils. *Childhood, 16*(4), 535–552.

Youdell, D. (2003). Identity traps or how Black students fail: The interactions between biographical, sub-cultural, and learner identities. *British Journal of Sociology of Education, 24*(1), 3–20.

Youniss, J., & Yates, M. (1999). Introduction: International perspectives on the roots of civic identity. In M. Yates & J. Youniss (Eds.), *Roots of civic identity: International perspectives on community service and activism in youth* (pp. 1–15). Cambridge University Press.

Youniss, J., McLellan, J. A., & Yates, M. (1997). What we know about engendering civic identity. *American Behavioral Scientist, 40*(5), 620–631.

Index

acquisition model of learning 8
aspirations 34, 43, 66, 67, 71, 79

capability theory 31, 70
citizenship education VII, 2–4, 7, 8, 10, 11, 24, 28, 30, 36, 38, 61, 63, 66, 69, 71
civic competences 8, 9, 18, 19, 33, 75

democratic forums 2–4, 32, 74, 75

elections 1, 2, 11, 13, 14, 17–19, 32, 34, 36, 74
enduring effect 10
equal access 3, 10, 37, 68, 75
ethnic composition 30, 36, 42, 44, 46, 50, 51, 53, 59, 60, 65, 74
ethnicity 34–36, 42–44, 46, 50, 51, 53, 55–57, 59, 66, 68–71, 79
excluded middle 67
exclusive clubs 3, 24, 61, 74, 75

gender 36, 37, 43, 44, 60, 67, 68, 71, 74, 79

International Civic and Citizenship Education Study VII, 3, 4, 13, 23, 35, 38, 39, 41, 42, 45, 61, 73, 77

ladder of participation 4, 7, 22
logistic regression 45, 50, 51, 55, 58, 64, 74

multilevel analysis 45, 47, 50, 53, 55, 58–60, 64, 74

normative justification 6, 7, 17, 23, 62

open climate 11, 12, 22, 23

participatory democracy 6
pedagogical justification 5, 7, 8, 12, 18, 22, 23, 62
political culture 25–27, 39, 41, 44, 45, 47–49, 55, 59–61, 63, 65, 66, 73
political engagement 1, 9, 10, 12, 30, 32–36, 64, 67, 69
political identity 9, 10, 20, 39, 70, 74, 75
political participation VII, 1–3, 7, 8, 10, 11, 22–24, 29–34, 61, 62, 66, 67, 69, 70, 73
positional 33, 58, 60, 65
private schools 29, 42, 51–53, 55, 60, 66, 74, 78
public schools 29, 42, 51, 52, 66, 74, 78

representative democracy 6, 7

school councils VII, 1–18, 20–27, 29–37, 40–43, 45, 47–71, 73–75, 77
social background 12, 22, 29, 33, 42, 71
SES composition 30, 33, 44, 50–52, 58, 60, 64, 65
social constructivist 8, 9, 11
social inequality 9, 12, 74
socialisation 8, 9, 11, 28, 31, 37, 62, 70, 71

voting 2, 10, 13, 18, 27, 34, 40

welfare regimes 26

www.ingramcontent.com/pod-product-compliance
Lightning Source LLC
Chambersburg PA
CBHW052051300426
44117CB00012B/2083